FALLOUT

Trudy Krisher

Holiday House / New York

On pages 15–16 the excerpt from "The Wreck of the Hesperus" by Henry Wadsworth Longfellow appears on page 1496 of *The American Tradition in Literature: Volume 1*, 3rd edition, edited by Bradley, Beatty, and Long (New York: W. W. Norton and Company, 1967).

On pages 24–25 the excerpt from "Fire and Ice" by Robert Frost appears on page 1083 of *The American Tradition in Literature: Volume 2*, 3rd edition, edited by Bradley, Beatty, and Long (New York: W. W. Norton and Company, 1967).

On pages 144–145 the excerpt from Act III, Scene II of *King Lear* by William Shakespeare appears on page 1092 of *William Shakespeare: The Complete Works*, edited by Peter Alexander (New York: Random House, 1952).

On page 197 the excerpt from "Tell all the Truth but tell it Slant" by Emily Dickinson appears in *Complete Poems* by Emily Dickinson, edited by Thomas H. Johnson (Boston: Little, Brown, 1960).

On pages 200, 202, and 205 the excerpt from "The Bells" by Edgar Allen Poe appears on page 801 of *The American Tradition in Literature: Volume 1*, 3rd edition, edited by Bradley, Beatty, and Long (New York: W. W. Norton and Company, 1967).

On page 220 the excerpt from "The Love Song of J. Alfred Prufrock" by T. S. Eliot appears on page 1276 of *The American Tradition in Literature: Volume II*, 3rd edition, edited by Bradley, Beatty, and Long (New York: W. W. Norton and Company, 1967).

On pages 280–281 the excerpt from "Dover Beach" by Matthew Arnold appears on page 904 of *The Norton Anthology of English Literature, Volume 3*, 1st edition, edited by M. H. Abrams (New York: W. W. Norton and Company, 1962).

"How Much Is That Doggie in the Window" on pages 306–307, is used with permission. Words and Music by Bob Merrill, Copyright © 1952 Golden Bell Songs, Copyright renewed 1980, Administered by Music & Media International, Inc., International copyright secured. All Rights Reserved.

Library of Congress Cataloging-in-Publication Data
Krisher, Trudy.
Fallout / by Trudy Krisher. — 1st ed.
p. cm.
Summary: The move of an unconventional Hollywood family to a
coastal North Carolina town in the early 1950s results not only in an
unlikely friendship between high school age Genevieve and newcomer
Brenda but also in a challenge to traditional ways of thinking.
ISBN-13: 978-0-8234-2035-3 (hardcover)
ISBN-10: 0-8234-2035-3 (hardcover)
[1. Prejudices—Fiction.   2. Friendship—Fiction.   3. North Carolina
—History—20th century—Fiction.]   I. Title.
PZ7.K8967Fal 2006
[Fic]—dc22
2006041193

To the dedicated reference librarians
at Wright Memorial Public Library,
who find the needles in my haystacks

Talons of wind clawed at the corners of the house as we huddled together inside the hall closet. My father struggled to tune in his shortwave radio. Against the screaming rain, my mother covered her ears, and I listened.

I heard the timpani of flying trash can lids. I heard the swishing snare drum of rain. I heard the drunken maestro of wind: tipsy at first, soon raucous and staggering.

Suddenly my father picked up a signal. "She's brushed Cape Hatteras."

I glanced at the hands on the windup clock. "Ten thirty," I announced.

"P.M.," corrected my father.

"That's only forty miles north of Easton," my mother wailed. Now she pressed her palms to her forehead.

I had known a hurricane was on the way. East Carolinians were schooled in the signs of approaching storms. First was the sight of shorebirds flocking inland; next came the stinging of salt in your nose and the tingling of the hair on your arms; after that, people stood outside their shops and sloops and studied the sky; then they began boarding up, taking in water and food and batteries. Finally, by the time the sea grass flattened against the dunes and the surf boiled, you had taken cover.

"Oh, dear," my mother cried, jiggling the telephone. "The phone's out."

"You know the phone's always the first thing to go, Martha."

"But George," she asked, plunging the phone on and off the hook, "how will we know Bud and Minna are safe?" Uncle Bud and Aunt Minna, my mother's sister, lived in a tiny house on the other side of Easton with my cousin Wills.

To escape their bickering, I concentrated on the rain hurling itself against the windows like monstrous sacks of rice, remembering that for me the first signal of a hurricane was always my father's flags.

Every August my father prepared for fall's hurricane season as if the end of the world were likely to occur that very year. First, he shook out his map and laid it carefully across the dining room table; on it were traced the routes of former storms that had threatened the North Carolina coast. The path of Hurricane Barbara, last year's August storm, was marked by an arc that just barely hugged the Carolina coastline. Finally, he put up the flags he had made himself out of weights and dowels and swatches of silk. During fall hurricane season each flag was carefully laid on the map as the radio reported the new latitudes and longitudes of gathering storms.

This year I had watched him monitor the approach of Hurricane Carol with his obsessive attention. A green flag marked the storm's development in the Bahamas on August 25. Each succeeding day was marked by another colored flag. As the storm drifted north and Carol huddled several hundred miles off the Florida coast, the flags turned a cautionary yellow. On August 30, the Monday when school was to begin, my father's flags showed the storm accelerating to the north-northeast: All the flags were red.

Now I struggled to curl up amid the cans of food and jugs of water crowding the closet. They looked like supplies for a camping trip. I was oddly comforted: Our family rarely did anything together. While the wind howled a demented lullaby, I pulled a blanket up over my shoulder and dozed.

"Power's down, Martha," my father barked, awakening me.

As I stirred, I heard the familiar drone of the air-conditioning dissolve. I read the dials of the clock glowing eerily in the darkness: 12:30 the hands read.

"Oh, dear, George," said my mother. "No phone. And now no power."

"You just expect these things in a hurricane, Martha," he shrugged. "I'm surprised we've had power for as long as we did."

"Well, in this modern world, George, you'd think—"

My father finished my mother's sentence. "Yes, in this modern world you'd think they'd have gotten better about their forecasts. Sometimes the weather bureau predictions are two or three hundred miles off course. Likely there are Communists fouling up the weather service, too. We ought to sic Joe McCarthy on them. That'd straighten things out."

In the darkness I shuddered, fumbling for a flashlight. When I switched it on, I was alarmed by how little light its circle cast, but my parents failed to notice. They were absorbed in their sharp-elbowed bantering.

I sighed and struggled to return to sleep, the flashlight flickering beside me like a ghostly night-light. I was tired of hearing about Communists. Daily, my father railed about them. I was tired of hearing about Joseph McCarthy, too. Since 1950 my father had hung on every word from the mouth of Senator McCarthy. Like the senator, my father believed that there were Communists in the State Department, Communists in the movie industry, Communists in the army.

While the flashlight cast a miniature moon and the wind wailed, I acknowledged that I was grateful to the Communists for one thing: Because of them, we now had a television set. My father had always been opposed to TV. "Television is no more than an electronic circus," he declared frequently. "You might pay to go to the circus now and again. You don't invite it to set up the big top in your living room." But that attitude had changed when my father heard that the Army-McCarthy hearings were to be nationally televised. Apparently Senator McCarthy had put the United States Army on the defensive, claiming it had been infiltrated by Communists. Now the army had launched an offensive against the senator, and my father had bought a TV set in April and sat transfixed before the flickering screen.

As the rain pelted the trees like a battering ram and the wind shrieked its lunatic howl, my father fiddled with the dials of his shortwave radio. Suddenly he caught a signal.

"They say the lighthouse's out at the point," he reported.

"What else, George?" my mother asked.

"Something about the shrimp trawlers up at the pier."

"What about them, George? What does it say?"

"Quiet, Martha," he ordered, annoyed now. The radio had begun to squawk like a parrot. He was losing the signal.

Even now while my father fiddled with the dials on his shortwave radio in the middle of a hurricane, my mother took up her favorite topic: something new that had to be purchased.

"George," she cooed, "don't you think a plant on a stand might look nice in that empty corner in the living room?"

My father ignored her. He kept adjusting his radio.

I heard the wind pick up and the tree branches slapping at the windows.

"George, dear," she repeated, turning her lips down, "that empty corner looks so bare. Don't you think it needs a bit of greenery?"

"Green," my father snorted, "is for grass, Martha. Green belongs outside."

As I listened to the storm, I thought about the greenery outside, remembering that both new pine and old oak were shredded like toothpicks during a hurricane.

I passed my mother the flashlight, hoping to distract her.

Now a clear signal came in over the radio, and my father looked alarmed: The Coast Guard station out beyond the marsh had lost its signal. So had the lighthouse at Pine Point. The winds had even blown out the anemometer at the radio station.

Suddenly we heard a cracking sound: It sounded like a gunshot.

"Oh, George," my mother fretted. "I'm afraid it's one of the big oaks in the backyard." She stood up as if she intended to go to the window to peer out into the yard, but then she sank down again as she remembered: My father had boarded all the windows up with plywood.

The cracking sound outside reminded me of that long-ago morning on the marsh when my father took me hunting. It also reminded me of my cousin Wills and his dog, Gunner.

Wills and his dog usually appeared on Saturdays, when my father and my uncle Bud grabbed either hunting or fishing gear and climbed into Uncle Bud's pickup truck. They'd hunt in the woods or fish in the streams, and they always returned home with something dead that made my mother shriek and my aunt Minna sigh with resignation. Then my father and Uncle Bud would spend the late afternoon cleaning the rabbits or fish over newspapers spread across the redwood picnic table in the backyard while my mother and Aunt Minna cooked.

While the men were gone, I spent the hours with Wills and Gunner, attempting to train Gunner for hunting.

Suddenly I gasped. I had heard a rushing and a rattling dangerously close to us.

"George!" Mother shrieked, fumbling for her husband's hand. "The roof!"

My father brushed her hand aside and reached for her flashlight instead. Slowly he opened the closet door to peer out in the direction of the roof. The closet door began to shake and tremble as if it might fly off its hinges.

I bit my lip and began to pray. *Deliver us from evil.* I had always prayed, ever since I was a child. Now I prayed for deliverance.

As the wind ripped erratically at the roof, I observed the regular pulse of my parents' breathing. As the rain pelted the sides of the house, the crackle of the shortwave radio soothed me like a crackling fireplace. And as the roof shuddered, my mother and father and I did something we rarely did: We grasped one another's hands.

2

Hurricane Carol had a single happy result: she had
put off the start of school.

Every year I resented the first days of school
because summer, my favorite season, had ended. Summer
meant Easton Beach, the place I had always loved. Not
because of the line of cars that swarmed to the beach like
ants to picnic tables. Not because of the promise of a pink
nose and brown arms and salt-bleached hair. Not because
of the string of blue cabanas dotting the shoreline like sap-
phires. I liked all those things, of course. But I loved the
ocean most of all for its *sounds*: the chattering of tourists
strolling the boardwalk, the splashing of lobsters diving in
restaurant tanks, the squawking of pelicans flapping their
wings beside the fishermen's catches on the piers.

And I loved the ocean for the way it made me feel
weightless. I moved gracefully through the surf, and I felt
powerful there: My feet pumped like fins; my head parted
the waves like a dolphin's snout.

I had written a poem about it, folding the scrap of

paper into my journal and stuffing the journal between the sweaters in my drawer.

> *The glassy blue sea*
> *is a mirror,*
> *a spectacle of*
> *turquoise,*
> *prussian,*
> *aquamarine.*
> *The sun*
> *glints off the lens,*
> *correcting*
> *the distortions of vision.*
> *Swimming into focus*
> *like a light-flooded windowpane,*
> *it reflects the spectrum*
> *of the*
> *unseen*
> *me.*

When I was younger, in the months from May to September, I had inhabited the deep blue world of the public pool that seemed another universe to me. But for the last two summers the public pool had been closed because of the polio scare, and even though my father's newspaper reported on the possibility of a vaccine, I knew I would still have to bear another swimless summer. My parents would never have permitted me to go to the beach alone, so my swimming, like my time with my journal, occurred in stolen moments. This year marked the first time I had ever willingly done something I was sure my parents would forbid.

I was especially dreading the start of school. This year was my first year in high school, and Sally Redmond, my best friend since grade school, had moved to Surfside Beach, New Jersey, at the beginning of the summer. I had missed Sally all summer long. Now I was anxious about walking through the doors of the high school entirely friendless.

I'd had intimations about how dreadful high school could be when I had helped Sally with her campaign for class secretary last spring. It had been a contentious election, for the winner would serve as our class's first high school representative in the fall. Sally had lost, but the campaign had introduced me to the gossip, rumor, suspicion, and secrecy that would, I feared, characterize high school.

A scene from only a few months ago had seemed like an omen.

Every spring a representative from the weather bureau visited each classroom in the Easton school system to teach about hurricane precautions.

Last spring a Mr. Harris had appeared with his charts

and brochures. He had held up two pictures. One showed a freshly painted house with a clipped green lawn and sparkling windows.

"You'd like your house to look like this—both *before* and *after* a hurricane, wouldn't you, boys and girls?"

A few of the students had nodded, but most sat sullenly silent. They hadn't liked Mr. Harris's *"boys and girls."*

When he had held up the second picture, we had seen that the same house had been transformed. The roof had been punctured by a tree trunk, windowpanes had splintered into spiderwebs, the yard had been strewn with upended trash cans and birdbaths, and splintered tree branches layered the lawn like a giant's idea of mulch.

In a whisper loud enough to be heard, Janice Neddeger had said, "That looks like Wilma's house *before* a storm."

Wilma Turner's face had flushed as she tried to squeeze her overstuffed frame more deeply into her seat.

I anticipated more such humiliating scenes in high school; without the security blanket of Sally, I was terrified of becoming their focus.

My friendless state was made more painful by my mother's constant references to it. Mother always liked girls who were "go-getters," a term that described herself better than her shy and awkward daughter. My lack of friends was one reason she had wanted the backyard swimming pool.

I had seen the building material catalogs that began arriving in the mail alongside my father's subscription to *Popular Mechanics*. He often consulted *Popular Mechanics* as he tinkered with his shortwave radio, his fishing rod, or his toolshed, all assembled from one of the magazine's many do-it-yourself kits. But I had never seen my father pore over designs in brick and concrete before.

While he studied his catalogs, my mother scurried about.

"Oh, George. Just *think*!" she exclaimed. "We can build a patio around the pool and get a real brick barbeque. And we can buy patio furniture, wrought iron chairs like they have up at Neddoger's. And Genevieve can finally have some *friends*!"

3

As I approached the doors to Easton High on a midweek Wednesday instead of a first-day Monday, I avoided deep puddles of water and stepped over uncleared tree branches. Only last week the bright blue letters of a huge metal sign read: WELCOME 9TH GRADERS TO EASTON HIGH. Now the sign was bent and twisted, buckled in the storm, and the WEL of WELCOME had been scattered somewhere by the wind. Only this blunt invitation remained: COME.

I had always been a good student, with the notable exception of math, and this year math meant Algebra I. I was terrified of failing my first math course in high school, especially because my father always pressured me about my math grades. My father was an actuary. Actuaries dealt with disaster. They assessed the risks of death, disability, accident, and sickness. Actuaries counted things: the number of highway deaths on Labor Day, the frequency of lightning strikes by state and month, the percentage of workplace accidents relative to numbers in the workforce. To an actuary, mathematics was not only the most important subject in the high school curriculum, it was the most important subject in life itself.

I was unafraid of English and history and science. In fact, I had been especially looking forward to my English teacher this year. The rumor was that Mr. Henderson was not only new to Easton but a first-year teacher as well. I stepped into the classroom and chose a desk as far away from Janice Neddeger as possible. My teacher's ready smile, overeager voice, and unworn suede on the elbow patches of his jacket confirmed his newness. As a novice, he began class by making an attempt at relevance.

"Given the weather we've experienced of late and the fact that our first unit of study will be poetry," he said, swinging himself easily onto the top of the desk, "I thought you'd be interested in how Longfellow described a violent storm."

Then he began to read a poem about a shipwreck. It was called "The Wreck of the Hesperus."

I liked the way Mr. Henderson threw himself into the reading.

Colder and louder blew the wind,
A gale from the Northeast,
The snow fell hissing in the brine,
And the billows frothed like yeast.

The breakers were right beneath her bows,
She drifted a dreary wreck,
And a whooping billow swept the crew
Like icicles from her deck.

She struck where the white and fleecy waves
Looked soft as carded wool,
But the cruel rocks, they gored her side
Like the horns of an angry bull.

I liked the images the poems contained. Even more, I liked the sounds made by the words and the way Mr. Henderson used his voice. I could feel the *i*'s of the misty snow "hissing in the brine" and the wind pushing through the *o*'s of "whooping billow." Listening to Mr. Henderson was like sitting on the shore listening to the ocean.

Mr. Henderson read us several sea poems that first day: *The Rime of the Ancient Mariner, A Visit from the Sea, Sea-Fever, The Chambered Nautilus.*

When he had finished, he picked up a piece of chalk and moved to the blackboard. He wrote the word *POETRY* in big capital letters on the blackboard. Then he said, "Get out some paper, please. I'd like you to write me a few paragraphs. Give me *your* definition of poetry."

I stared at the blank page in front of me. The other students were writing furiously in a first-day-of-school frenzy.

I scribbled a few things on my paper.

"Emotion."

Everybody thinks of that, I told myself.

"Words that sound right together."

Not really. It is more than just sounds.

"Remembered feelings."

Not exactly.

"Insight."

Maybe, I told myself. *But insight's not unique to poetry. History and fiction and philosophy and other things besides poetry produce insight, too.*

Then I scratched everything out. My pencil tore a hole in the paper.

"Poetry can't be defined," I wrote quickly, in a rush. "It's too mysterious." The other students' pens were racing across their pages. I couldn't think of anything else to write.

While Mr. Henderson collected our definitions, he went on, like all first-year teachers, about the joys of learning that awaited us. "Later in the term we'll be reading literature about the future," he said, mentioning books like *Brave New World* and *1984* and stories by people like H. G. Wells and Jules Verne. "We'll be reading about traveling in time machines and diving thousands of leagues under the sea," he enthused, hoping, I was sure, that his own enthusiasm might light a fire under the damp logs that were his students. I wondered how long it would take before the eager smile sagged, the excited voice grew clipped, and the new jacket was replaced by a comfortable old sweater.

Just then Mr. Henderson was interrupted. A new girl had appeared at the door. She was tall, taller than me, taller than most of our classmates. I noticed that the mass of soft, round black curls on her head was at odds with the pair of black glasses that scratched a ruler-straight line across her eyebrows. From the glasses up, she reminded me of a jack-in-the-box, wound tight and suddenly sprung.

"I just arrived," she announced matter-of-factly, in a way that said school rules like being on time were invented to be excused.

"Yes, you did," Mr. Henderson agreed, nodding his head in a first-year-of-teaching attempt at humor.

No one laughed.

"I'm new to Easton. My folks and I just arrived in Easton this morning. The roads were washed out in some places. We just now pulled up in front of the school."

"Well, then," Mr. Henderson began, "you and your family missed a memorable experience of Easton's fine weather." His eyebrows lifted in a hopeful attempt at humor.

The new girl heaved a sigh and rolled her eyes. "Ha, ha. Very funny," she said. Unlike the rest of the class, she didn't hide her annoyance with his lame joke.

"Have a seat," Mr. Henderson said, motioning her to the empty seat in the back of the classroom.

After that, our new teacher had a bit of trouble regaining his footing. I saw it as a sign of inexperience. Veteran teachers dealt with interruptions like one of those old-fashioned telephone operators, connecting an assortment of incoming interruptions with calm and dexterity.

Now Mr. Henderson cleared his throat. "Since we'll be looking at *other* people's ideas about the future this term," Mr. Henderson said, "I want you to begin by thinking about your *own* ideas. Your first assignment—due tomorrow—will be a report to the class about your own personal vision of the future."

I tried not to take the assignment as an omen: At our house, the vision of the future was bleak.

4

The next class was social studies. Mrs. Pagano, my new teacher, laid her hands on the classroom globe and spoke of the anxiety that was spreading to all the corners of the earth. Then she turned from the globe to focus on the huge map of the world. I jumped at the snapping sound of the map being pulled from its slot on the wall.

I kept my eyes fixed on the tip of Mrs. Pagano's pointer. The map of the world was divided in half, into two large land masses, one green and one red. The green masses seemed friendly and welcoming, as if they belonged somehow to me myself, for those masses represented countries allied with the United States of America. The red masses, however, seemed forbidding and frightening, for they represented those countries allied with the Union of Soviet Socialist Republics, the USSR. I understood that the USSR was an enemy that wished to destroy my own country, an enemy that had nuclear missiles pointed at American cities like the arrows on my father's hurricane maps.

Mrs. Pagano's map frightened me. It marked a foreboding that seemed to reach beyond my father's maps. It underscored my family's gloomy vision of the future.

Mrs. Pagano chatted casually about herself. She explained that the scrape she was wearing came from her summer trip to Mexico. She laughed that her husband had finally insisted that she stop wearing lederhosen to the grocery store after one summer trip to Germany. I liked the relaxed and easy manner of Mrs. Pagano. Unlike some of my former teachers, she didn't take herself too seriously.

Now she passed out a newspaper. The black-and-white newsprint reminded me of my father.

Mrs. Pagano said, "We have just looked at the map of the world. Now we will read in your *Weekly Reader* about something called the Cold War."

I shivered. I knew about the Cold War. Perhaps that was what I had been experiencing of late. Something chilly. Something cold. Something with enemies all around. "Better dead than Red," my father always said.

Suddenly the new girl's hand shot up. I hadn't even noticed that she was also in my social studies class.

"Yes?" Mrs. Pagano asked. "I'm sorry that I don't know everyone's name yet. Give me a few days."

"Brenda. Brenda Wompers," the new girl said with an assurance that proclaimed her silly-sounding name with confidence. "How can you call it a *war*?" Her wide forehead thrust forward as she emphasized the word *war*, and

Brenda Wompers's black-rimmed glasses slipped down her nose. "There are no troop movements, no blackouts."

I thought it was rude the way Brenda looked at Mrs. Pagano suspiciously through the tops of her glasses. That look reminded me of aging secretaries with thinning hair who sullenly handed back forms that you had filled out incorrectly. The new girl seemed bent on causing problems.

But Mrs. Pagano responded calmly to Brenda. She had years on Mr. Henderson. "You are certainly right, Miss Wompers. The Cold War is a very different kind of a war. There are clearly no air-raid sirens blaring overhead, no casualty figures in the daily newspaper. Yet, as your *Weekly Reader* explains, the Cold War is a war nonetheless."

I glanced over at the red and green map at the front of the classroom. Thinking about the Cold War made me uneasy, for I imagined the U.S. and the USSR as two unruly bears rising up on hindquarters, jaws dripping, paws feinting, poised to attack. One false step, and the Cold War could turn into a hot war. If that happened, the Russians and the Americans would incinerate each other with nuclear bombs, and the whole entire world as well.

Burying my nose in the *Weekly Reader*, I thought about my father. He was a newspaper reader, the cover-to-cover kind. Because he was also a man of few words, for whom grunts and mumbles passed for conversation, I remembered a breakfast table conversation that summer I turned ten.

"Well, Martha," my father announced over the pages of newsprint. "You'd do well to mark this day. June twenty-fifth," he said, "nineteen fifty."

"Why is that, George?"

My mother only marked her calendar with sale dates and bridge club meetings.

"There's another war in the Pacific now," my father said. "North Korea has finally invaded the South."

My mother stood at my father's elbow, staring down at him blankly. "More coffee, dear?" she asked, refilling his cup.

My father rattled his newspaper pages and turned to me. "Well, *you* know what that means, don't you, Genevieve?"

I was grateful that my father didn't wait for my reply. He merely thrust his serious face more deeply into his newspapers.

I also remembered the conversation that took place two years later, when I was twelve.

My father had risen from his chair at the dinner table. I had never seen my father rise to speak before. From my sitting position, I recognized how tall he was, how thin.

"The world will never forget this day, ladies," he announced to his audience of two. "November first, nineteen fifty-two, is a date for the history books. We Americans have exploded the first H-bomb," he said, pausing for effect. "Over the Marshall Islands."

The impact of this news was diluted as I struggled to identify the Marshall Islands. Were they in the Atlantic or the Pacific? Were they somewhere near Hawaii? I couldn't place them in pictures in any of my geography books.

"The bomb wiped out an entire island. It no longer exists."

I was confused. I was uncertain about whether to feel happy or sad. I was sad about the destruction of the island, of course. But I was oddly relieved that there would be no need for me to identify the Marshall Islands on a geography test now. They would have to strike the Marshall Islands from the geography books forever.

Now, swimming up from my reverie, I studied the *Weekly Reader* pictures of Russian leaders like Joseph Stalin and Nikita Khrushchev. I looked over graphs comparing U.S. grain production with Soviet grain production. I scanned charts contrasting the number of nuclear warheads in America with the number of nuclear warheads in Russia. Then I was halted by a sidebar. It contained a poem called "Fire and Ice" by a man named Robert Frost.

Some say the world will end in fire,
Some say in ice.
From what I've tasted of desire

I hold with those who favour fire.
But if I had to perish twice,
I think I know enough of hate
To say that for destruction ice
Is also great
And would suffice.

Would the world end in fire, blasted into ruination by the nuclear enmity between the Americans and the Russians? Or would it end in ice, the world frozen by hatred, numbed by the icy pinpricks of the Cold War's fear and loathing? Which end would be worse?

Now I heard Mrs. Pagano's instructions, and I was strangely comforted by them. "After you have finished reading the article on page three," she said, "I want you to begin responding to it in your journals. And I'll collect the journals from you on Friday."

5

I kept glancing at the clock, willing its hands to freeze like the hands of our clock at home when the electricity went out. But the hands on the classroom clock sped along as Mr. Henderson checked his attendance list, stacked some papers, and closed the classroom door.

It was Thursday, the second day of school. When Mr. Henderson called for volunteers to share their ideas about the future, I squeezed the ring in my pocket and slunk down in my seat. One thing was sure: I had not produced an impressive vision of the future for Mr. Henderson.

Janice Neddeger volunteered to go first. I should have expected that. She was always the first one to call attention to herself. When she ran against Sally for class secretary, she bragged that her grade point average was a solid B when it was actually a high C rounded up. Claiming that she herself hadn't really been interested in running, Janice hinted broadly that her friends had forced her into it.

I shouldn't have been surprised, either, with what happened next. Janice called all of her friends up to the front to stand beside her. "We decided to make it a group effort, Mr. Henderson," she said, swirling a long brown ponytail from her left shoulder to her right and smiling at our first-year teacher.

Janice Neddeger never traveled alone. She was like a sultaness carted on a pallet by members of an entourage that fought to gain the privilege of holding her aloft. Her group always included Iris Campbell, April Summers, and Renee Fedders, but Sally and I discovered that it easily expanded to include whoever was currently being seduced by her charm.

I watched Janice and almost all of the other girls approach the front of the classroom in their identical scuffless saddle shoes. I saw the identical checkered scarves around the necks of each girl, each scarf carefully square-knotted and slanted to the left.

Suddenly I missed Sally Redmond.

Janice Neddeger held up a poster board. THE WONDERS OF THE ATOMIC AGE, it read. The block letters of the poster had been colored in blue, each one outlined carefully in silver.

Suddenly I realized that the girls had worked on the signs together at Janice's house.

Without me.

I had been to Janice's house once last year, a few

months before the spring election. Sally and I had been invited to the overnight party Janice Neddeger held to celebrate her thirteenth birthday.

Everything about Janice's house seemed new and up-to-date. After the new hi-fi finished blaring Bill Haley's wildly popular "Rock Around the Clock," Janice replaced it with a record by a new singer from Memphis named Elvis Presley, whom Janice had recently discovered. Listening, I heard a musical defiance that was decades apart from the bubblegum sweetness of my Pat Boone records, the only songs permitted on my ancient record player. After the music ended, Janice introduced us to the latest party game. We girls lay on the floor while Janice put nickels on our noses, instructing us to wiggle them off without using our hands or shaking our heads; soon giggles were ricocheting across the living room. After Janice's parents went to bed, we huddled under the blankets with flashlights, ogling the latest copy of her brother's *Playboy* magazine. The next morning as we left, Janice promised we'd be invited to watch the Miss America Pageant in the fall. One thing was certain: By September I'd know whether I'd been invited to this birthday party only because of lively and energetic Sally.

Now Janice Neddeger began her report. "Atomic energy," she announced, "promises a future more bright than we ever could have imagined." When Janice smiled, I noticed that she had straight, even teeth. "Atomic energy is just like Columbus's discovery of America. It represents the discovery of a whole new world for everyone on the planet."

The familiar revulsion I felt for Janice Neddeger surfaced again. She was alluding to Sally's campaign theme from last spring. Janice had produced an image of the earth sliced in half vertically. The left side of the globe was colored in green; the right side of the globe was colored in red. The slogan atop the planet read: "Better NEDdeger than REDmond." Sally and I had thought it was a shameless tactic. We had countered with an image of our own. Attempting to turn Janice's claims on their head, we had used the same picture of the earth, but without the red and green polarities. Our planet had displayed the earth's calming blue color. "Discover the Whole New World of High School—Sail Away with Sally for Secretary," our slogan had read.

Next, April Summers stepped up, holding one end of a clothesline in one hand and passing the other end to Iris Campbell. The girls stretched the line from one corner of the room to the other.

I caught Mr. Henderson's neatly trimmed mustache turning up with pleasure.

"Brad," Janice Neddeger asked coyly, "can you help us?"

The other students giggled. Brad Connors was Janice Neddeger's boyfriend, and someone I had never liked.

Brad shuffled up to the front of the classroom, his long arms hanging awkwardly from his broad shoulders, his boyishly handsome face seeking direction from Janice. Janice held up a toy car. The car had a large metal ring inserted into the roof. Janice placed the toy car in Brad's big hands, leading him to the end of the rope held in April Summers's fingers. "Go ahead," she ordered the big boy. Brad slipped the toy car onto the end of the rope by the metal ring. Janice turned to the class and beamed as if her handsome boyfriend had just done something astonishingly clever. Then April and Iris lifted the ends of the clothesline up and down like a seesaw, and the car zipped back and forth along the rope.

"In the future we can imagine atomic-powered cars suspended from overhead tracks," Janice pronounced to her awestruck classmates. "They'll never have to stop for refueling."

A scattering of applause flitted through the room. Mr. Henderson made notes in a small spiral-bound notebook he held in his hand.

Then Renee Fedders stepped forward holding up a poster-board picture of a modern house. Thick arrows had been drawn to point at its sides and roof.

"The future will offer climate-controlled atomic houses," said Janice, "heated and cooled by walls of radioactive uranium."

Now Marion Ramsey moved to the front of the classroom. She had a toy stethoscope draped around her neck. She held up a set of beakers in a wooden rack. Each of the beakers had been filled with a different colored liquid. I imagined the girls at Janice's house squealing with delight as they took turns with the eyedropper and different bottles of Mrs. Neddeger's food coloring.

"We'll have atomic medicine," gloated Janice. "We'll have radioactive isotopes locating cancer for treatment."

Marion then stepped away, and Carol Calloway took her place. Carol was carrying a basket. As Janice spoke, Carol pulled items from the basket.

"We'll have fruits and vegetables grown with light supplied by U-235," said Janice.

Carol held up a head of cabbage. "And the food will be cooked instantaneously in microwave ovens," Janice added, grinning.

"We'll even have atomic energy vitamins and atomic toothpaste," said Janice. Carol held up a pill bottle and a tube of Colgate toothpaste. "No need to brush twice a day ever again."

Janice gave a sweeping motion with her small, neat hands. Suddenly half the boys in the class stepped up front with her.

I sank farther down in my chair. I saw that after Janice's presentation, only a few students would be left to offer their views of the future. I fingered the ring in my pocket. I had borrowed it from my cousin Wills as a last-ditch effort at a report. Wills would no longer be attending school this year. He had dropped out. He had finally finished eighth grade after a few tries, and Uncle Bud and Aunt Minna had agreed that school was no longer something Wills had to endure. Generously, without hesitation, Wills had loaned me the ring that was his special treasure.

Aunt Minna had ordered the ring for Wills over half a dozen years ago. Wills had seen it advertised on a Kix cereal box. For fifteen cents and a box top, Wills had received the futuristic atomic-viewer ring that every boy in his neighborhood now owned. Wills had seen things in that ring that I failed to see: the sealed atom chamber and the gleaming aluminum warhead and the place for secret messages. But I knew what Wills had really seen as he held that ring tenderly and passed it to me: a time that seemed long ago, a time when he could hope to be just like the other boys.

"In the future we'll even have atomic weather," Janice announced, the center of her group of friends at the front of the room.

Bobby Owens said, "We'll be able to melt the poles with atom bombs and have warm seasons all over the world. No more winter."

April Summers held up a poster on which an atomic cloud covered a melting ice cap.

Link Palmer added, "We'll have artificial atomic suns lighting the planet all day. No more night."

Carol Calloway held up a poster of the planet Earth bathed in sunlight.

Adam Morrison, our grade's star pitcher, added, "No baseball game will be called off on account of rain."

The class laughed.

Doug Haskell said, "No more hurricanes like the one we just had. We'll just use the power of the atom to blast them off into the ocean."

Everybody cheered.

I looked around the classroom. Nearly everyone was up at the front of the room. Only me, Eddie Brinkley, shy Wilma Turner, and the new girl—her arms folded angrily across her chest—were left. I caught the frown on Mr. Henderson's face. He had been counting, too, "I'm concerned," the teacher began. "It's not clear to me that you boys did much work to prepare your part of the report. It looks to me like you may be riding along on the coattails of the girls. Are you sure you boys worked on this part of the report yourselves?"

"Oh, yes, sir," Brad Connors lied.

It was clear as a bell that the boys hadn't done a lick of work. I was glad Mr. Henderson hadn't been fooled.

Janice Neddeger defended the boys. "We all got together to work on this last night," she said. "At my house. We adapted my brother's car and cut the clothesline and made the posters and assigned our parts."

Mr. Henderson listened thoughtfully.

I imagined my classmates at Janice's house. Although I knew the boys had let the girls do most of the work, I

33

was also sure that they had had fun. Mrs. Neddeger had probably provided lemonade and allowed them to push back the furniture while they danced. Mr. and Mrs. Neddeger weren't anything like my own parents. Over the years I had invited a number of girls to visit, but the experience was always uncomfortable. The plastic over the furniture was bad enough, but the hovering presence of my father, suspicious of any loud giggles or hoots, was even worse.

Sally had made things easy for me. She never pressed for an invitation to my house. She was always comfortable to invite me to hers. I had a standing invitation for Monday night. At nine sharp, Mrs. Redmond handed the two of us a bowl of popcorn, Mr. Redmond passed us an afghan to wrap around our knees, and Sally snapped on the television set. I watched, spellbound, as the title of the show—*I Love Lucy*—was spelled out in ribboned letters.

I especially loved the family shows like *The Adventures of Ozzie and Harriet.* I liked the way those families talked to each other. When the children on those shows gulped their dinners or talked out of turn, their parents kindly winked at each other over the centerpiece. Most of all, I had noticed the way the TV families tolerated surprise: the welcoming of a stray dog shown up on the doorstep or an extended visit from a long-lost great-aunt. In my family, surprise was to be avoided.

Those TV families were nothing like my own.

"Besides," said Janice, interrupting my reverie, "it felt good to get everyone together after that horrible hurricane. The assignment, Mr. Henderson," she said, "helped us get through the first nerve-racking day of high school."

Mr. Henderson pursed his lips and nodded, considering her explanation. He looked over at the four of us who were still sitting in our seats. Obviously, Janice had not gotten "everyone" together after the hurricane. As I stared at Janice Neddeger, I thought about the lyrics to "Shake, Rattle, and Roll": *You look so warm but your heart is cold as ice.* I wondered what my teacher was thinking.

"Well," Mr. Henderson sighed, "I have to agree that this was a very creative approach to my assignment. We'll have time later on in the year to talk about group projects and how the work is best distributed. Your report, students, clearly spelled out a vision of the future. I thank you for your perspectives."

Suddenly everything was turned upside down. The new girl stood up. She was almost as tall as Brad Connors. And she was furious. The eyes behind her glasses were angry slits. Her face was red.

"Too bad," she shouted, "it's all a lie. Too bad it's all just a bald-faced lie!"

I wondered how our first-year teacher would handle *this* challenge.

As it turned out, the fallout from the arrival of the new girl lasted all year long.

6

The atmosphere in the cafeteria at noon was as free-wheeling as the deck of a pirate ship. Mrs. Pagano had lunch duty, and above the shoulders of her serape, she craned her neck in all directions like a periscope, alert to mutinous behavior.

I sat alone in the cafeteria at lunchtime. I listened to chair legs scraping the linoleum, to the lid on the ice-cream chest thumping open and closed, to plastic trays banging against the aluminum rails of the serving line.

Everyone else seemed to have a friend. Sitting alone, I thought about Sally Redmond. In my mind's eye I began a poem about memory. About how memory allowed you to feel the presence of someone, to both enjoy and miss them at the same time.

I caught the title on the cover of a textbook next to a lunch tray: *Understanding Geometry*. Geometry was something I expected would be impossible to understand. But I wouldn't have to face it until next year. If, that is, I managed to pass algebra.

Now Iris Campbell approached the other side of the table. Iris was wearing her hair in a ponytail like Janice Neddeger's. If Iris saw me across the table, she didn't acknowledge me. "I had that new girl in my physics class," Iris announced disgustedly. Iris was the only one of Janice Neddeger's friends that was on the honor roll. Iris took all advanced courses like advanced English and advanced algebra. Now she had remarked that she was taking advanced physics this fall as well. "The new girl kept bragging about where she was from," Iris said. "California. Over and over. California."

"She did that in geometry class, too," offered another girl. "Only she pronounced it 'Cal-i-*for*-nia.'" I heard the girl stretch out the word so it sounded like a long Hollywood limousine.

"And she just butts in all over the place," Iris grumbled. "In physics class Mr. Reuthven announced that we'd work on special science topics of our own choice. Things like unexplained mysteries. Like what causes earthquakes. Or the Bermuda Triangle. Stuff like that. He said he wanted us to see if the laws of physics could explain any of them. And that new girl just butted in and took my topic. *I* wanted to do the one on flying saucers," whined Iris. "But she just grabbed it up first."

I knew a little bit about flying saucers. Most folks in Easton did now. Last spring several people in Easton had claimed to see UFOs—or unidentified flying objects, as they called them—off Easton Beach. Everybody in Easton had an opinion about them.

I knew there'd been sightings all over the country for the last few years, too. There had been strange disks zipping up and down Mount Rainier in Washington State. The summer before last there'd been sightings of flying objects by airline pilots around Washington, D.C.

Janice Neddeger had even claimed to have seen a flying saucer. She and Iris Campbell were the only ones to have seen it. Janice had wrecked her father's car on an April evening last spring, having secretly taken it out for a spin. She had run it into a telephone pole near the beach, blaming the accident on the distraction of a mysterious object flying overhead. No one would have believed her except for the picture Iris had taken of the saucer. Iris's picture had been blown up and plastered across the front page of the *Easton Eagle,* making believers out of most Eastoners and calming Janice's angry parents. Afterward, Janice had hobbled around on crutches for a few days, nursing a sprained ankle and generating a few sympathy votes for the election.

"And that new girl kept talking all through class," Iris went on. "Asking questions nobody was interested in. Except for Mr. Reuthven, of course," Iris said. She had gnawed an apple all the way to the core.

"But Mr. Reuthven kept encouraging that girl," Iris complained, tossing the apple core onto a paper napkin.

Her fingernails were painted in Coral Vanilla, the same nail color that Janice used. "Everybody found her annoying," Iris complained. "And Mr. Reuthven kept saying we were lucky to have someone bringing us new scientific ideas all the way from California."

"Cal-i-*for*-nia," mimicked a tenth-grade girl, picking up her American cheese sandwich made with two slices of white bread.

While the other students laughed, a familiar shame swept over me as I stared at the lunch my mother had packed. Her determined work as a Tupperware saleswoman always crept into my lunches. At home, all of our food was stacked neatly in cupboards, decanted into pastel Tupperware containers. The Ritz crackers were crisped in the Tupperware cracker box; the Maxwell House coffee was preserved in the Tupperware coffee container; the Creamettes spaghetti was sealed in the Tupperware pasta jar. My mother also fussed over my school lunches. Each item was in a separate plastic container, the point being to keep my lunch hygienic and sanitized by separating the carrot sticks from the cottage cheese and the tuna fish from the apple slices. I longed to be like the other kids who munched peanut-butter-and-jelly sandwiches from paper sacks flattened by fannies on the school bus.

The other students finished eating, wadding up napkins and stuffing waxed paper into paper bags. I looked around at the white tile walls, at the gray Formica tables, at the aluminum bins and trash containers scattered around the cafeteria like miniature weapons silos. The colors were institutional and cold. They made me shiver. I recognized that I didn't understand much about physics or geometry, but that I did know one thing: I'd prefer the world to end in fire than in ice.

7

On Friday of the first week of school, Mrs. Pagano showed a film about the Russians. The film showed pictures of cities with roofs shaped like onions, with farms blanketed with snow like thick layers of white dust, with soldiers stomping in heavy boots over frozen ice, their breath sending wispy trails across the frigid air. I understood that Russia was our enemy; yet when the camera zoomed in on the faces of the Russian people, I saw heavyset men and women in frayed coats that looked like I often felt: desperate to get out of the cold.

After the film, while Eddie Brinkley rewound the film on the projector, I began scribbling my thoughts in the margins of the journal Mrs. Pagano required us to keep. I somehow couldn't forget about the shivering Russians in coats as thin as baking papers. The thoughts kept me busy for most of the rest of the period.

It was Friday, and Mrs. Pagano collected these journals as she had promised. In these notebooks students were supposed to reflect on the textbook, the classroom discussions, the film, the *Weekly Reader* articles, or anything else that appealed to us. The notebooks made a leaning, multicolored tower on top of Mrs. Pagano's desk. While we read our *Weekly Reader*s, Mrs. Pagano read through the notebooks and made marks inside.

Suddenly I was startled by the sound of my own words coming from the front of the room. Disbelieving, I saw Mrs. Pagano's mouth moving above the yellow cover of the notebook I had just turned in. Frozen in my seat, I studied the head of my teacher bent over my notebook. Mrs. Pagano was reading the lines from the poem I had been attempting to write:

Russian faces: pale as dough.
Eyes glazed with exhaustion.
Black teeth like raisins in the batter.
Russian bodies: limp-limbed from
Kneading a living.
Fingers stiff with cold.
Arms thrust into
Coats thin as baking papers,
Hungry for the warmth of ovens.

Mrs. Pagano grinned with pleasure when she had finished reading, but I was trying to swallow a mixture of anger and humiliation. My poetry was something private.

Mrs. Pagano called after me when class dismissed.

"Genevieve," she began, "if I acted hastily . . ."

But I had hurried away. I kept my head down as I dodged bodies on the way to my next class.

The next class was a class designed especially for ninth-graders this year. It was one of those Civil Defense classes I was familiar with from junior high, and it met only one day a week. My father explained that these classes had been the good idea of President Truman; they had begun under his Civil Defense Administration.

I remembered the animated films and the booklets with images of friendly rabbits taking cover in holes beside windows being blown out. I remembered pictures of slow-witted turtles withdrawing into their shells to avoid flying glass. To me these pictures and their warnings seemed as familiar and routine as the hurricane precautions I had learned about year after year.

The teacher this year, however, was a Civil Defense officer with googly eyes and spit-shined shoes that squeaked across the linoleum floor. He spent the first half of the class reading from a government pamphlet. Atom-splitting was just another way of causing an explosion, it explained, and the chance of survival was the same as for everyday accidents. The pamphlet made clear that people were already bombarded each day by harmless radiation from cosmic rays.

He spent the second half of the class passing out tags for us to wear. The Civil Defense officer said that the military-style tags were something school boards all over the country were issuing to students to help parents identify their children in the event of a nuclear bomb. As I lifted the chain over my head, I felt a sudden chill.

Suddenly the new girl was on her feet. "Tell me, sir," she began. "Why do we need a dog tag to identify us if a nuclear bomb is no more harmful than a simple explosion?"

I stared at Brenda Wompers. She was leaning forward, shifting her weight from foot to foot like a boxer.

I watched the Civil Defense officer open his pamphlet and sputter an incoherent response.

"And what about the H-bomb?" Brenda cried. "Doesn't the recent H-bomb test change everything?"

The Civil Defense officer blinked his googly eyes. My classmates stirred. I remembered that my father had mentioned something about this H-bomb test over his newspaper last spring, but I couldn't remember the exact facts.

"You know, sir. The H-bomb test," she said in the face of the officer's blinking eyes. "At the Bikini Atoll. The one that was a thousand times bigger than the bomb dropped on Hiroshima."

I wondered how this new girl seemed to know so much.

"Bikini," Brenda now said, looking around the classroom, anticipating the effect of her words. "*Bikini*," she repeated. "Don't all of you think it's well named?"

Brenda was speaking directly to the class now. My classmates had begun to snigger.

"Well, I think Bikini is a perfect name for the test site. After the H-bomb blast," she said, throwing up her hands, "that island was stripped naked. It was barely wearing anything at all!"

The students laughed, poking each other in the ribs.

"That's enough," the Civil Defense officer ordered.

But the new girl wasn't finished. She began to spout out all kinds of information I'd never heard of before: facts about American uranium mines, about the production of fissile material, about the nuclear activities in places as far flung as Oak Ridge, Tennessee, and Billings, Montana. In just a few moments Brenda Wompers had spouted more facts about nuclear weapons production than I had learned in all of the classes I had ever taken.

I felt frozen with fear as I listened to the new girl shout about meltdowns and Geiger counters. I recalled the Bible passages of Revelations that prophesied the end of the earth marked by fire and blood and wild beasts. I prayed silently, determined to ask Reverend Steward about the passages in Revelations at my next confirmation class.

"With all due respect, sir," Brenda said, winding down, "isn't there just one fact we need to know about nuclear war?"

The Civil Defense officer swallowed hard. His Adam's apple moved up and down in his throat. "What's that?" he asked, falling into her trap.

"Isn't the only fact we need to know about nuclear war the fact that *we can't survive it*?"

The classroom descended into chaos. The Civil Defense officer had lost control. After he stumbled out of the room, teachers from neighboring classrooms appeared to restore order in time for the all-school drill that took place once a week and was timed for the end of our Civil Defense class.

These were duck-and-cover drills to prepare us for nuclear attack. Sometimes the drills required us to place our heads on our desks and cover them with our arms. Sometimes we had to crouch under our desk. In elementary school these drills had seemed harmless. Now, somehow, on the heels of Brenda's outburst, they seemed more serious. Today as the siren sounded, the drill sent us to the basement, where we crouched near a wall and shielded our faces.

As I huddled among the aluminum heating ducts, my hands covering my eyes, I heard a harsh whisper in my left ear.

"She had no right," the whisper declared.

Now I cracked my fingers and peeked at the floor below me. A pair of sandals was aligned to the left of my saddle shoes.

"Mrs. Pagano had no right to read your poem without your permission."

Now I stared into the face that went with the voice. I

had taken in the black-rimmed glasses already, but I hadn't been close enough to see that the eyes behind them were a deep, warm brown fringed with lashes that were thick and dark. Brenda Wompers's nose was as straight-sided as a triangle. Only the end was crooked, and it slanted eccentrically to the right.

"She should have asked you first."

I felt something easing inside me: Ice cubes loosened from their trays.

Suddenly Brenda changed the subject.

Now she bugged out her eyes in imitation of the googly-eyed Civil Defense officer. "Scary, isn't he?" she said, flinging her fingers wide before her glasses.

I jumped back, startled. Then I choked back a giggle.

"Maybe," I allowed. "Maybe not." One of the rules of high school was never to admit what you were really feeling.

Then Brenda whispered conspiratorially, the black frames of her glasses against my ear. "Well, I think he's pretty silly," she stated boldly. "But I know someone who really *does* think that silly man and his silly lessons are scary. Someone you'd never suspect. Wanna guess?"

I scanned the floor of the basement. My classmates were hunched against the basement walls like soldiers in bunkers. They all looked frightened to me. I shook my head. "I dunno."

"Brad Connors."

I stifled a laugh. I was sure Brenda couldn't have been

right about that. Although I'd always hated the way he'd treated Wills, Brad Connors was the most admired boy in ninth grade. For one thing, he was the biggest boy in the whole school. He had broad hulking shoulders and wore triple-E shoes. For another, the varsity football coach was trying to draft him from our junior varsity team.

"How do you know?" I asked.

"The broken pencil," Brenda said. "You can't see him from here," she went on, "but when the siren sounded, Brad Connors put his pencil between his teeth on the way to the basement. I heard a snapping sound. I think Brad Connors clamped down so hard, his pencil might have snapped in half."

The all-clear sounded, and the students rose. On the way up the stairs, all of a sudden Brenda raised her arm and gave a hollow heating duct a swift smack. The sound was like two metal garbage can lids played as cymbals. Startled, some of the students shrieked, some giggled; then they went stomping up the stairs, roaring with laughter.

Back in the classroom, I slithered into my seat. From across the room, I caught Brenda Wompers gesturing at me. Catching my attention, Brenda pointed in the direction of Brad Connors.

Gripped in the big boy's fist were the two halves of a broken pencil.

Then and there, I decided that there might possibly be something to like about Brenda Wompers.

After the storm had passed, our yard was a muddy swamp with downed tree limbs and yard debris. The ceramic gnome from the Wilsons' house had sailed over into our yard; it was turned on its head in the spot where I hoped to find a diving board one day. I wouldn't mention the pool to my father, of course. But I could see that any work on it could only follow major efforts to clean up after Hurricane Carol.

As I combed loose twigs together with the rake on Saturday afternoon I thought back to the conversation I had had with Mr. Henderson on Friday. He had asked if I might stop by his classroom before leaving for home.

"I thought you might be interested in these," he had said, passing me a piece of paper filled with handwritten lines. "Mrs. Pagano told me you wrote well. I also liked the way you attempted to define poetry for that in-class reflection. I thought you might be interested in some more attempts to define poetry. Naturally, we didn't have time in class to cover all of these."

I remembered all the definitions of poetry Mr. Henderson had written on the board. I had been struck by how difficult it was to define things, how elusive and sometimes even painful.

I remembered back to that word they had called Wills: *retard*.

Wills, seventeen to my fourteen years, was a sweet boy-man that Aunt Minna called special and that the kids around Easton called a retard.

What had that word meant? Was a *retard* a person who couldn't read as fast as the others? A person who struggled to get out of junior high school? Or was a *retard* a person who was somehow different from the others, a person whose difference had been regarded not as a commonplace idiosyncrasy but defined as an extraordinary peculiarity?

As I had been musing, Mr. Henderson had been smiling. "I want to try to encourage those few students with an eye for poetry," he said.

I felt the redness rising as it often did whenever someone paid attention to me.

"Thank you," I said.

I had read the list of additional definitions on his paper over and over so often that I now knew them by heart.

"Poetry is the best words in their best order."
—Coleridge

"Poetry is a way of taking life by the throat." —*Frost*
"Poetry can communicate before it is understood."

—*T. S. Eliot*

*"Poetry is the spontaneous overflow of powerful
feelings."* —*Wordsworth*

"Poetry is the rhythmical creation of beauty." —*Poe*

Despite my wandering mind the yard work had gone quickly. I had now gathered a tall pile of broken branches. I fetched an empty trash can from the garage and began dumping the branches into it. Even though the work was tiring, I was grateful: It gave me time to think about all that had happened at my mother's Welcome Wagon meeting. This morning Brenda Wompers's mother had been a guest.

My mother was president of the Easton Welcome Wagon Club, an organization dedicated to helping new neighbors feel at home in the community. New neighbors were a fact of life in Easton. Easton was beginning to grow, expanding from its traditional industry of fishing into the more modern industry of travel and tourism. Moving vans plastered with the names of companies like Bekins and National Van Lines were now a more frequent presence in neighborhood driveways. But the people who moved into our neighborhood with their identical furniture and identical appliances and identical new-model cars reminded me of Janice Neddeger and her friends. I was always grateful for the unusual sighting of a rusting vehicle or fenceless yard. I had always liked discovering what was unique about our neighbors: that little Patsy Early was just learning to ride a tricycle; that Mr. Borchers leaned on his rake for a long chat every fall; that Miss Simmons worked for days on the homemade candy she gave out at Halloween. Like those who believed in UFOs, I liked the idea that the unusual was somehow possible.

Every few months Mother hosted Welcome Wagon meetings in our home, and in the days leading up to these meetings, she engaged in furious housecleaning: polishing the furniture with paste wax, deadheading the flowers in the border, holding glasses to the light to scan for spots. Mother dressed carefully for these events, notching her sequined cinch belt a notch tighter than was comfortable.

"After all, Genevieve," she cooed, polishing her Welcome Wagon president's pin until it gleamed, "each new neighbor's a potential Tupperware hostess." Her pin was emblazoned with the words "Neighbors All" against the image of a Conestoga wagon.

A Welcome Wagon meeting began as the Welcome Wagon members stood in a circle to welcome whatever new neighbors had joined the Easton community since the last meeting. The circle harked back to the pioneer days when the covered wagons arranged themselves in a circle for protection and community. As they came through the door, new neighbors shook hands around the circle, engaging in getting-to-know-you chatter, sampling recipes from the latest women's magazines, and receiving business cards from local bankers, doctors, lawyers, and insurance agents.

Patricia Wompers, like her daughter, dressed indifferently. There were no cinched waists or box pleats, no ruffled crinolines or petticoats like those featured by the designers in my mother's magazines and worn by my mother's friends. The buttons down the front of Mrs. Wompers's blouse had been aligned unevenly, one placket longer than the other. Her mane of gray hair had been gathered at the back of her neck and fastened with a decidedly unfashionable rubber band.

Mrs. Wompers raised as much curiosity at the Welcome Wagon meeting as her daughter had at school. Most of the new neighbors over the years had come from New Bern or Wilmington or Morehead City, communities not far from Easton. Perhaps a few had come from Raleigh or Charlotte, but no one had ever moved to Easton from as far away as California.

"And what did your husband do there?" Nancy Summers had asked.

"He worked in the film industry. In Hollywood."

Our living room had flooded with silence. Most of my mother's friends had husbands who managed grocery stores or repaired fishing boats or owned shops on the boardwalk.

"My!" my mother had exclaimed. "Did he ever know anybody famous?"

"Oh, yes. Harry knew Lucille Ball and Desi Arnaz quite well, and he met Milton Berle at a party once."

My mother's friends had studied Patricia Wompers carefully.

"And why did you ever leave?" Yvonne Campbell had asked.

"Oh, Harry and I just wanted a simpler life. Hollywood's a real pressure cooker."

The Welcome Wagon ladies had to think about that.

"Did you have a swimming pool?" I had heard my mother ask. On more than one occasion, she'd hinted to her friends that my father was building us a backyard swimming pool. "I hear everybody in California has their own pool."

"Yes, we did, Martha," Mrs. Wompers had said, "but I'm afraid we didn't use it much. Ultraviolet rays are bad for your skin. I'm afraid public opinion has yet to catch up with science."

A long silence had followed.

"And what will your husband do here?" Nancy Summers had asked. Mrs. Summers's blue stiletto heels exactly matched the powder blue shade of her blouse.

"Well, Harry and I will run the souvenir shop up on the boardwalk," Patricia Wompers had said. "Together," she had added firmly. "As partners."

Mrs. Summers had looked surprised. She was not familiar with husbands and wives working together as business partners.

I knew about the souvenir shop. Elderly Raymond Donner had been eager to retire for years. I heard he had finally sold the shop.

"Do you have any children, dear?" Mrs. Fedders had asked.

"Yes," she had said, smiling. "One daughter. She's a ninth-grader up at the high school."

"Did you hear that, Gen?" my mother had asked, tapping on my pink-sweatered arm. "Have you met Mrs. Wompers's daughter yet?"

"I think she might be in my English class," I had muttered warily.

"Well," my mother had offered, "Gen can acquaint your daughter with the way things are done among the young people here."

As I had passed a plate of tea biscuits, I had admitted that I hardly knew myself how things were done among young people in Easton, and much of what I knew, I didn't like. Last spring, at the end of the school year, Sally and I had been attending an overnight at April Summers's house. After dark a few of the boys had called through the windows, daring us girls to sneak into the amusement park at the end of the boardwalk. We had climbed onto the Ferris wheel and rocked back and forth in the seats, swinging wildly against the deep black night. We had broken into an ice chest and made snow cones for ourselves out of shaved ice and candy-colored sugar syrup. But when the boys began to paint names on the haunches of the horses of the carousel with cans of black paint, Sally and I had scurried away. When I had heard my father read about the incident in the *Easton Eagle,* I acknowledged a contradiction: I both wanted and didn't want to remain a part of this group.

I was hot now. I sat on the stoop to rest and thought about what else I knew about Mrs. Wompers's daughter. I knew she had broken the school dress code.

At school yesterday morning, Mr. Gillis, our home-room teacher, had simply pointed to Brenda with one fat finger that held a piece of chalk. Rudely, like a drill sergeant, he barked: "You!"

Brenda had looked around, unsure at first whom the teacher meant.

"Yes, you," Mr. Gillis had ordered. "Up." The chalk stub was shaped like a bullet.

When Brenda had risen, I had seen that she was wearing blue jeans and a T-shirt. I had known only skirts were permitted by the school dress code; I had wondered if Brenda did.

"Your clothes," Mr. Gillis had said, his hands shooing at the words like flies. A streak of yellow chalk had run across the crease of his crisply pressed trousers. "You're in violation of the dress code, young lady."

"Oh, I didn't know," Brenda had replied. "In California we never had anything as dumb as school dress codes."

The room had fallen silent. The word *dumb* had hung in the air. So had the word *Cal-i-for-nia*.

Mr. Gillis's fingers had curled tightly around the yellow chalk. "Ignorance of the law is no excuse," he had said. He had begun to pace across the front of the room.

Then Brenda had thrown her shoulders back. Under her T-shirt the points of her shoulder blades had looked like two spears. "A dress code is hardly a *law*."

The class had gasped.

"My father was right," she had huffed. "He told me I'd have a lot less freedom here. He said that the South would be different from *Hollywood*." When Brenda had pronounced *Hollywood*, she had rolled the word slowly out of her mouth, spinning it haughtily like a film star.

The class had sniggered. Now they planned to enjoy this outsider's angry discomfort.

"I suppose I'll have to dress differently tomorrow," Brenda had said. "May I sit down now?"

"No, young lady," Mr. Gillis had replied, his words like fists in her face. "You will dress differently *today*. You will report to the principal's office, call your parents, and change your clothes before you are allowed back into school."

As she had gathered up her things, I saw that Brenda's shoulder blades had turned from sharp to sagging as she carried herself quietly to the doorway. But a final act of rebellion had defied any sense of defeat. Once she had stepped across the threshold and out of the doorway, she had lifted her leg and kicked the door shut with a fierce thrust of her foot.

Even Mr. Gillis had jumped at the sound of the slamming door.

The yard work seemed to take forever. I continued to rake the branches scattered under the big oaks. While I made a new pile for the can, I remembered the special ceremony that had ended the Welcome Wagon meeting. The women had gathered in a circle, each one repeating the mantra "Neighbors All," like a litany recited in church. Normally, after each brand-new neighbor departed, my mother and her friends stayed behind to gossip, and today was no exception.

As soon as Mrs. Wompers had left the Welcome Wagon meeting, my mother and Eloise Neddeger and Nancy Summers had begun their discussion: Had anyone noticed the sandals she wore instead of stylish heels? Had anyone understood that crazy business plan, which included adding used books to the merchandise in the souvenir shop? Had anyone understood a single word on those brochures Patricia Wompers passed out as she left?

Eloise Neddeger had said, "I heard they're getting rid of the boardwalk store's penny-candy bins."

"Why would they ever do that?" my mother had asked, a look of horror flooding her face. "Ray Donner took in half his income from children with a sweet tooth."

"And I hear they're keeping cats in there, and some kind of bird, too," Yvonne Campbell had said.

My mother had replied, "Well, it'll be *somebody's* duty to call the health department."

On parting, Mrs. Wompers had given each member of the Welcome Wagon Club a gift. Fumbling over a big straw bag, she had pulled out dozens of spiny conch shells. I had seen shells just like them piled up in Mr. Donner's boardwalk shop.

"These arc my favorite things in our store," Mrs. Wompers had announced. "Marine biologists and historians have taught us a great deal about conchs, haven't they?"

Silence had draped the living room like a curtain.

Mrs. Wompers had continued to speak. She had rattled on about the wonders of the conch and its shell: its uses as meat, as tool, as ornament, as object of trade.

"Well, then," Mrs. Wompers had sighed, "perhaps their presence in your homes will inspire you to learn more."

Afterward, my mother had grumbled about the way this cheap present with its pointy edges would scratch the finish on her furniture. She had tossed it out in disgust, but I had retrieved it, slipping it into the drawer beside my bed. At night I would hold it to my ear in the darkness, listening to the rushing sounds of the sea. It was something else I kept hidden from my parents this year.

By now I was tired. My hair was filled with twigs, and my back and legs ached from bending over and snapping branches. I was grateful to see Aunt Minna and Wills and Gunner arrive to help clean up our backyard. They had lost part of their roof in the storm, and my father and Uncle Bud had spent several days hammering plywood over the gaping hole and rescuing the interior of their home from water damage.

I was always glad to see Aunt Minna. Aunt Minna had cheeks as round as buttery rolls, and the fleshy folds of her body made her easier to hug than my straight-edged mother.

I was even gladder to see Wills and Gunner. Wills had loose lips surrounding a wide drooling smile; he had ears that stuck out at sharp angles like the locks on Aunt Minna's Mason jars. I thought he was handsome in his own special way.

I knew what people said about my cousin. How he couldn't learn to read. How the only job he could get was cleaning the cages of the hamsters and birds at Petty's Pets over by the beach. But to watch Wills with Gunner was to know that Wills was the smartest young man in the world when it came to animals.

Mr. Petty had come to trust Wills to do more than just

clean out the cages. Wills was now feeding the animals and grooming them. Mr. Petty had taught Wills to give them the medicines they needed, too.

Wills had only had Gunner since last winter. He had found him as a stray scrounging through the trash at the amusement park.

Uncle Bud hadn't been sure about the dog. On the first Saturday visit after Wills had rescued Gunner, Uncle Bud had complained that dogs were expensive and a lot of trouble.

Aunt Minna had nudged him. "Now, Bud," she had said, "give the boy a chance."

My mother thought Minna spoiled Wills. I thought Minna just loved him a lot.

"Have you found out what kind of a dog it is, Wills?" Uncle Bud had asked.

"A yellow Lab," Wills had said.

"Is that a hunting kind of dog, Son?" his father had asked.

Wills had nodded. "A retriever."

Then Uncle Bud had looked at my father and nodded. "I suppose if you could train it to hunt in the marshes, we just might be persuaded to keep it, wouldn't we, George?"

My father had slapped his brother-in-law on the back and nodded.

"What's the name of that critter, Son?" Uncle Bud had asked.

"If you're planning on hunting with him, we could call him Gunner," Wills had said.

The two men had nodded. Gunner it was.

The first time Gunner had been taken out to the woods and heard a rifle fire, he had bolted away.

"Better name for him might be Ol' Yeller," Uncle Bud had said, shrugging his shoulders in the direction of the disappearing dog.

I had been there when Wills had first introduced Mr. Petty to Gunner. The black macaw had been squawking in the background and the litter of new kittens had been mewling in their box, but I had heard Mr. Petty as plain as day.

"A shy dog's harder to train than a mean or aggressive one," Mr. Petty had said. "If you want to learn to train a dog, you'll surely cut your teeth on this one, Wills."

But all summer I had helped Wills patiently train Gunner.

Wills took two thick square boards to clap together to mimic the sound of gunshot. First, Wills backed farther and farther away from me until I could just barely hear the sound of the clapping boards. Then, Wills got me to stand by Gunner with a treat as he clapped the boards together from far away. When the dog stayed still as the sound was made, I slipped a treat into Gunner's muzzle. Then as Wills gradually brought the clapping sounds closer and closer to the animal, I was prepared with a treat when the dog stayed still. Gunner was hardly ready for a hunting trip, but Wills and I had made some progress. The dog loved the way each practice session was rewarded by a swim.

Those swims in the ocean had made the summer more bearable.

It helped that Wills worked nearby at the pet store on the boardwalk. I was allowed to bike to the beach, five miles from my house, on the ruse that I would visit Wills. Occasionally I had retreated to a secret spot at the beach, an abandoned lifeguard station that sat high on tall, crane-like legs, partially obscured by the shifting dunes and far away from the wooden crossovers favored by tourists. From the lifeguard station I had scribbled lines about the sea grasses waving like anemones and the hermit crabs carrying their shell homes on their backs like hoboes' rucksacks.

Even with Wills's company I was tired of working in the yard. Picking up a metal trash can lid, I motioned to Wills to pick up another lid. Together we struck up a back-yard band, crashing our metal cymbals together, bent double with laughter.

My mother stuck her head out the back door. "Get to work, you two. Stop that horsing around." I caught Aunt Minna's face beside my mother's. Hers was grinning while my mother's was frowning. "The sooner you finish, the sooner we get George Hardcastle to work on that pool."

Quickly I put down my metal lid. What she had said was motivation enough for me.

9

So much had changed this year in such a short time that I took great comfort in the things that had *not changed*. High school still ended at three thirty, the same time the junior high was dismissed. I was happy that each day still began with the Pledge of Allegiance, the only change this fall being the insertion of *under God* between *one nation* and *indivisible*. And I was especially happy that Sunday afternoons after church still meant confirmation class. Even if it meant skipping the weekly pancake breakfast at the diner.

Wills and I always arrived first, hovered over by Aunt Minna as Uncle Bud and my parents said good-bye and headed for the diner and our after-church breakfast of pancakes with syrup without us.

Sometimes I resented having Wills in the class, for I wanted to seem just like all the other students, and Wills was a reminder that I was the girl with the retarded cousin.

Sometimes I felt touched by the foolishness of Wills's

mistakes. Everybody I knew was singing the Bill Haley tune "Shake, Rattle, and Roll," but Wills always referred to it as "Roll, Rattle, and Shake." And even though *The Adventures of Superman* was Wills's favorite TV show, he could never remember the everyday name of the "real" Superman. It was never Clark Kent; to Wills it was always Kent Clark.

Looking over at the framed words of the Beatitudes, I felt ashamed. "Blessed are the merciful, for they shall attain mercy," I read, praying for forgiveness for the times I had found Wills annoying or an embarrassment. Studying Wills's slack smile, I felt angry with myself: Wills had always been dear to me; the fact that I wanted more independence from him now that I was in high school didn't mean I loved him any less.

I studied the map of the Holy Land while the class members filed in. The map took up an entire wall in Reverend Steward's study. When I was a child, our Sunday school class had taped paper dolls to the map to mark special places in the Holy Land: a baby in swaddling clothes to identify Bethlehem; a boat filled with Jesus and his disciples to identify the Sea of Galilee. Now we had been given geography tests that challenged us to identify Judea, the Sinai desert, and the missionary journeys of Paul. We had memorized the Ten Commandments, the Beatitudes, and the Apostles' Creed. I struggled to help my cousin Wills with all of this work. Sometimes I succeeded.

We also met twice a month after church for discussions with Reverend Steward.

"So," the reverend began this week's class, "I believe we decided last time to take up another good question raised by Scripture."

I watched Janice Neddeger, April Summers, and Renee Fedders arrive together late, slipping into empty seats in the corner of the room. Reverend Steward nodded in greeting.

"The question is," he asked, "who is my neighbor?"

I had always loved Reverend Steward's questions. They were so much better than the questions you were asked in school. At school the questions had one-word answers: *Columbus* discovered America; *have* is a *verb;* the *numerator* sits on top of the denominator.

I thought hard about his question. But in confirmation class a familiar routine took place. Week after week Reverend Steward began the class by asking a question, and week after week the room then filled with an awkward silence. It was just like school.

Reverend Steward repeated his question. "Who is my neighbor?"

Again, no one answered, so the next familiar part of the routine took place: Reverend Steward called on someone. I always hoped it wouldn't be me.

"Wilma," the reverend said, turning to Wilma Turner,

a girl even shyer than I. "What about you? Who is your neighbor?"

Wilma peeked out from under her watchful eyebrows. "Mr. Donner, I suppose," the girl said.

Mr. Donner lived next door to Wilma and her widowed mother. It was his souvenir shop that Brenda Wompers's family had bought.

"Thank you, Wilma," Reverend Steward said. "And do you have any special *obligation* to Mr. Donner as your neighbor?"

Link Palmer quipped, "No loud parties, Wilma," he said, mugging for other students such as Janice, April, and Renee.

Wills joined in the laughter that followed, grinning stupidly. But I winced. Parties were not part of Wilma Turner's life, and Link knew it. I'd disliked Link Palmer for a long time. He, along with Brad Connors, had been one of the boys involved with Wills on that day of special shame so long ago.

"Well," Wilma offered, brushing her limp hair from her forehead. "Maybe during the storm," she stammered. "Mama and I tried to help Mr. Donner out. We offered him to stay in our house with us. He didn't want to, though."

"Is that all?" Reverend Steward asked, addressing the rest of group. "Is that the only obligation Wilma owes to her neighbor Mr. Donner? To offer him shelter during a storm?"

Silence fell. Reverend Steward was not getting any-where.

He rose from the Windsor chair and moved to a big pad of paper mounted on an easel. "Well," he said, "let's list all the things that Mr. Donner might need. We'll go around the room. Starting with you, Link."

Link frowned. As Reverend Steward moved around the room from student to student, the paper on the easel began to fill up with suggestions: driving to doctor, cutting grass, buying groceries, raking leaves, cleaning up yard after storms.

When Reverend Steward arrived at me, it seemed that everyone had already made most of the possible sugges-tions.

I looked into Reverend Steward's eyes. They sparkled with a kind of hopefulness.

"Perhaps we could just visit with Mr. Donner," I said. "Talk to him. I'm sure he gets lonely all by himself."

"Thank you, Genevieve," Reverend Steward said, his face flooding with light. "Mr. Donner might have more than just physical needs." Reverend Steward was writing the words "just talking" on the thick pad of paper.

"Perhaps," he added, "Mr. Donner might have spiri-tual needs, too. Perhaps he might enjoy someone read-ing the Bible to him. Could we add 'reading the Bible' to our list?"

While some of the students nodded, I saw Janice and

Renee roll their eyes. They couldn't imagine themselves reading the Bible to Mr. Donner. I couldn't, either.

Now Reverend Steward returned to his chair. "Let's turn to Scripture, shall we?"

Wills rose quickly, eager to help. He passed out the classroom Bibles from the wheeled cart in the corner of the room, only dropping one.

"Let's find Matthew 25:35, shall we?"

I helped Wills find the passage in his Bible. Then I found the passage in my own Bible.

I had loved reading the Bible as a child. Often I found the stories themselves confusing, but I loved the sounds of the words written there.

Reverend Steward had us read the passage responsively. First he read a line, then we read a line. I liked this technique. It helped me listen more carefully to the words.

"I was hungry and ye gave me . . ."

"Meat," chorused the students.

"I was thirsty and ye gave me . . ."

"Drink."

"I was a stranger and ye . . ."

"Took me in."

Then Reverend Steward stopped and paused. "What do you think Matthew is saying? Does *neighbor* mean *just* the person who lives next door?"

I liked his question.

"Gen, you've been doing well on this subject," Reverend

Steward said. "What do you think? Is Matthew implying that we have a spiritual obligation to treat *everyone* as our neighbor?"

"Perhaps," I stammered.

Now Link Palmer spoke up. "But that's ridiculous. Does that mean we have to be good to a murderer? a thief? a Communist? Don't you have to draw the line *somewhere*?"

Janice Neddeger piped up. "Yeah. With Brenda Wompers," she stated flatly.

Everybody rolled their eyes knowingly.

"I don't understand," Reverend Steward confessed.

"She's that creepy new girl at school," Renee added.

"Yeah," said Iris. "She asks questions all the time. She takes over the classroom."

"She dresses funny. She wears sandals instead of saddle shoes."

Huddling beside her in the basement during the civil defense drill, I had seen not only the sandaled feet but the hem of her rolled up jeans peeking out from under the long skirt that covered them. Brenda had returned to school, honoring the dress code in fact, but not in spirit. Inside, I had quietly saluted her.

"She thinks she's better than us. She brags about being from California and how dumb Easton is compared to it."

The gossip and rumor mill, I saw, was in full force, just as it had been against Sally last spring before the student elections. When Sally had eaten lunch with the friendless kids like Wilma Turner and Eddie Brinkley, Janice spread the rumor that Sally was buying votes. When Sally surveyed some of our other classmates about their worries about high school, Janice accused her of using fear to garner supporters. When Sally challenged Janice to a debate before the election, Janice fiddled with the truth: Sally, she said, was a person who just liked to hear herself talk.

"Well, I can see where you might find a lack of *modesty* objectionable," offered Reverend Steward, "but what about clothing? If Jesus walked in here today, what would He be wearing?"

Silence.

Reverend Steward smiled. "Don't you think *He*'d be wearing sandals? And a long, funny-looking robe? Indeed, people might say Jesus looked odd, too. Would that keep us from considering Him as our *neighbor*?"

Reverend Steward sat forward in his chair. "Do the Commandments have anything to say about this?"

I went through the Commandments silently.

"What's number nine?"

The answer came immediately: *"Thou shalt not bear false witness against thy neighbor,"* I blurted out.

The other students stared at me while Reverend Steward nodded.

"And what was the shorthand version of the Commandments, people? You know, if you have too much trouble memorizing all *ten,* what are the two that Jesus considered most important?"

I looked over at Wills's face. It had sparked like a fire-cracker. "Love God," Wills blurted out.

"And the second?" asked Reverend Steward.

Now Wills was flummoxed. He wrinkled his brow. He looked up in the air as if the answer could be snatched from somewhere right above his head.

Then his face brightened again. "Love your neighbor."

Reverend Steward added, "Yes, love your neighbor— *like yourself.* Thank you, Wills."

Wills beamed. I wanted to stand on my chair and applaud.

After class I was confronted by Janice Neddeger.

"Why didn't you come over to work on our report about the future, Gen?"

I saw Janice wink at Iris Campbell as she asked her question.

I stammered, "I didn't know I was invited." I could feel the redness rising in my face like it did every time I was thrown off guard.

"We left a message with your mother," Janice purred. "Didn't she give it to you?"

Now she favored me with a half smile. "Do you think you're too good for us?" she asked. Then she quickly turned away.

I was sure Janice was lying about the invitation. I knew

my mother. She was desperate for me to be the kind of go-getter girl who was regularly included with the other girls. My mother would never have forgotten to give me a message like that.

I watched Janice's retreating back and forgot entirely my questions for Reverend Steward about the end of the world. All I could remember was what we had talked about in confirmation class this afternoon. We were supposed to consider each person as our neighbor.

That meant Janice Neddeger was supposed to think of girls like Brenda Wompers and me as *her* neighbors.

But it meant I was supposed to think of Janice Neddeger as *my* neighbor as well.

10

After church and pancakes was my weekly breath of freedom. Wills cleaned the cages and walked the dogs at Petty's Pets on Sunday afternoons, and I was sent with him as a kind of babysitter, although around animals Wills hardly needed supervision. Once his chores were finished, Wills and I were free to roam the boardwalk or the beach until Uncle Bud picked us up. Since Uncle Bud was invariably late, we often spent our Sunday afternoons exploring Easton Beach.

Today, my mother asked, "Genevieve, dear, would you run this gift basket over to Patricia Wompers? She left it behind after the meeting yesterday. Even though it's a Sunday, the shop might be open. After all, they're trying to get Mr. Donner's shop ready for business."

As my mother looped the gift basket over my arm, I asked, "By the way, did Janice Neddeger happen to call in the last few days?"

My mother's eyes brightened. "No, why?" she asked. Too eagerly.

"Just wondering," I said, hearing the car door close behind me.

As I dropped Wills at the pet shop I studied the basket on my arm. Every new neighbor received a Welcome Wagon basket. The basket was filled with gift items from local merchants: a shiny green trowel from Peter Rabbit's Nursery, a jar of orange marmalade from Delights and Delicacies, a coupon for a bag of fresh dinner rolls from Scoggins' Bakery, an Irish-linen tea towel from The Emerald Isle Gift Shop on the boardwalk. Others of the ladies had donated gifts they made themselves: Mrs. Millikin's loose tea packets, Mrs. Perkins's crocheted toilet roll cover in the shape of a lady's bonnet. My mother always offered a newcomer a free Tupperware Wonder Bowl and an invitation to host one of her plasticware parties.

I loved walking the wooden steps to the boardwalk, the boards clomping under my feet. I loved the line of candy-colored storefronts that sold a welter of products like bait, bathing suits, lemonade, ice cream, diving gear, and fishing poles. My favorite stores were at opposite ends. They were Petty's Pets, where Wills worked, and the souvenir shop, which the Womperses now owned.

In Mr. Donner's souvenir shop, I'd had fun watching the out-of-town vacationers studying postcards over their sunburned noses, exclaiming over the gulls carved atop pieces of driftwood or the sand dollars in clear plastic bags. I liked seeing the tourists buying the big plastic key rings that said "Welcome to Easton, North Carolina." The key rings and the pennants and the bumper stickers made me feel proud. Perhaps in some small way the world might come to hear about tiny Easton, North Carolina, after all.

I climbed the set of rickety steps that led to Mr. Donner's shop. From what I had overheard at my mother's Welcome Wagon meeting, Mother didn't care for Mrs. Wompers. Was that why she was sending *me*?

My hand hesitated on the doorknob. Then I twisted it and pushed.

"Top o' the mornin'. Good *day*," a raw voice squawked.

I looked up and saw a bright-eyed parrot in a cage that hung from the ceiling right over the door. "Skeee-*waaack*!" he said, rustling his blue-green feathers.

I looked around at what had been the familiar souvenir shop. The candy bins had been pushed to the back of the room. The three-sided glass display cabinet had been piled with what looked to be cast-off clothing. In the floor space behind the display case sat mountains of books that threatened to cause a small avalanche. The familiar revolving racks of postcards and sunglasses and hurricane maps had been pushed to the side. A black cat that had been sleeping atop a clothing pile jumped from his napping place and moved toward me, swirling his sleek body around my ankles.

"Can I help you, young lady?" asked another voice, a human one. The voice also came from near the ceiling.

Across the room I saw a thin and bookish-looking middle-aged man atop a ladder in a corner. I heard his careful footsteps rattle the aluminum steps as he climbed down to greet me.

"Trish! Brenda!" he called out. "We've got a visitor!"

Suddenly Mrs. Wompers and Brenda appeared from the back of the store. I recognized Mrs. Wompers from the Welcome Wagon meeting. I didn't recognize Brenda at first. She was wearing a baseball cap pulled tightly over her black curls; she could have been mistaken for a tall and scrawny boy.

"Good *day. Eeeeee*-awk!" the parrot squealed. Now the parrot flew from its cage to settle near the cat, atop a pile of discarded clothing. I hadn't realized that a bird and a cat could behave as friends.

"Hush, Silver," Brenda said, approaching me. "That's Long John Silver," she said, introducing the parrot. "Dad let me adopt him from a movie set. Don't let him scare you," she said. "He's got a big mouth." Then Brenda grinned. "Like me."

I shifted awkwardly on my feet.

"Here," I said to Mrs. Wompers. "You forgot your gift basket yesterday."

"Oh, dear, yes," she apologized. "I can get so absent-minded at times. And I was flustered about meeting everyone and then learning so much about the weather," she said, tossing her thick gray halo of hair.

It had been a predictable Welcome Wagon meeting in that respect. New neighbors were curious about the storms and hurricanes that threatened the Carolina coast, and my mother and her friends were eager to acquaint them with Carolina weather stories.

"You can expect downed power lines," Yvonne Campbell had said.

"But then there are things that manage to surprise you," Nancy Summers had said. "After Hurricane Carol, Al and I found a stingray swimming in our pond!"

I had watched Mrs. Wompers's mouth twisting as she struggled to remember all of the advice she was being given: boil plenty of water, check the batteries in your radio. I had remembered one sign of an approaching storm that rivaled my father's hurricane maps: My mother always scrubbed the bathtub with extra care and then filled it to the top with water.

"Harry and I entirely missed the storm, thank goodness," Patricia Wompers had confessed to the other Welcome Wagon members. "We'd stopped in Illinois at the World Council of Churches meeting. They're calling for the destruction of all nuclear armaments."

I had seen the look of dismay pass from woman to woman, like disapproving glances at a tray of stale tea cookies.

"When we got to the shop, we saw that a good deal of the inventory had been destroyed by the water." Mrs.

Wompers had moaned in genuine distress. "How do all of you manage to *cope*?"

"You just *learn* to cope," Blanche Millikin had said.

Now Brenda interrupted my reverie. She said, "My mother was shocked by what she learned at the Welcome Wagon meeting. It hardly ever *rains* where we come from in California."

I admitted to myself that I was also growing a little tired of hearing about California: its film industry, its superior weather, its gifts of parrots from movie sets. A tiny part of me sympathized with the gossip that was circulated about Brenda.

Now I held the gift basket out and watched Mrs. Wompers take it into her hands.

"Oh, how lovely," she said, eyeing the goods inside. "Our thrift shoppers will be delighted to pick up some of these linen towels."

I watched Mrs. Wompers rooting through the gift basket, piling its contents atop the cast-off clothing as the black cat scooted off. Didn't she know that linen towels were to be hung in the bathroom when guests were expected? Wasn't she interested in discovering for herself the pleasures of Mr. Scoggins's homemade rolls topped with a gift of fancy marmalade? Did she prefer giving away the Tupperware bowl to keeping it for herself?

Brenda explained, "See all these clothes here, Gen?"

I scanned the piles of old skirts and galoshes and jackets

across Mr. Donner's display counter. You couldn't miss them.

"We're going to stock a thrift section over there," Brenda said, pointing to the south wall. "Mother saw the need for it as we drove into Easton from the west. The houses there look a lot like the barrios in Los Angeles."

I knew about the poor people who lived west of town. They swept up the amusement park, ran concessions on the boardwalk, picked up trash along the beach. I swallowed hard, remembering Reverend Steward's discussion about neighbors.

"By the way, Gen," Brenda now asked, flipping off the baseball cap and running her fingers through her shiny black curls, "would you like to stay and help?"

Mr. and Mrs. Wompers nodded eagerly at her suggestion.

"Well, perhaps," I said. "But I'll have to check on my cousin in a little while."

I helped Brenda organize the bins and counter and racks.

"Are you really getting rid of the penny-candy bins?" I asked Brenda.

Suddenly Mr. and Mrs. Wompers stopped their sorting. They had overheard my question. The serious faces they turned to me reminded me of the tragedy masks on theater marquees.

"Science is clear about candy, Genevieve," declared Mrs. Wompers.

"Sugar does a person absolutely no good," her husband replied.

"Rots the teeth. Corrodes the body," said his wife.

"But Trish and I won't get rid of the candy bins right at first. We need to get the community used to the kind of store this will be. You know, educate people. We'll start by moving the candy bins to the back. But we're clear about one thing: Those candy bins will eventually be discarded."

I felt the nagging voice of guilt whispering inside of me. I had enjoyed Mr. Donner's coconut patties. First the chocolate melted on your tongue; then the coconut dissolved into the chocolate, forming a sweet, syrupy pool in your mouth.

Now both Mr. and Mrs. Wompers struggled to navigate a huge oil painting across the room. Mr. Wompers was on one side of the painting; Mrs. Wompers was on the other.

Brenda pointed to the north wall. "See that space over there?" she said. "We're going to try to collect some art from local artists and sell it in here."

I stared at the immense canvas that now rested against the west wall.

Mr. Wompers asked, "What do you think of our painting there, Genevieve?"

I cleared my throat. The canvas was streaked with black and yellow and white blobs as if paint straight from the tube had been squeezed onto it. "It's very nice," I mumbled.

Then Brenda marched to the north wall and draped her arm across her father's shoulder. "I think it *stinks*, Dad," Brenda said. "It could have been painted by a monkey. Gen probably thinks so, too. Only she's too polite to say so."

Suddenly Mr. Wompers's sober mouth broke into a smile. "Spoken like a woman with a mind of her own," he replied.

I was surprised by the brash way Brenda had talked to her father. I was even more astonished at Mr. Wompers's reaction.

Now Mrs. Wompers explained: "We encourage Brenda to speak her mind. After all, Harry and I believe in speaking *our* own minds. Why should we deny this right to our *daughter*?

"And by the way, Genevieve," Brenda's mother continued, "we're not too happy with what that high school of yours thinks about speaking one's mind."

I felt torn. *"That high school of yours."* Was it really *mine*?

"And I'm not too happy with the curriculum, either," Mrs. Wompers went on. "In California our Brenda was in a gifted program. She had plans to be a physicist," she added.

Mr. Wompers beamed. "Just like her mother. Did you know, Genevieve, that Brenda's mother worked on the cyclotron at the Ryan Institute in Glendale?"

I shook my head. I had never known a mother who worked. Or a physicist, either. In fact, I wasn't sure what a physicist did.

Mrs. Wompers concluded, "It seems that the Easton schools don't believe in offering special programs for special students."

I got quiet. What Mrs. Wompers said was true. Wills had never been enrolled in any kind of special program. His educational experiences had consisted of two things: being made fun of and being ignored. The kind of special programs he needed were only available in bigger towns like Raleigh and Winston-Salem.

"Easton's approach to education," Brenda piped up, "is to make sure that everybody is *equally* bored."

Brenda was stroking the cat *and* the parrot, both animals sitting calmly at opposite ends of a pile of clothing. I marveled at the odd wonderland of this shop, where poor people were provided with affordable clothing and birds and cats got along.

"Well, Harry and I intend to make our views known up at your school. Brenda's gifted in mathematics and science.

And we object to that Civil Defense program she's required to take, too. It's sheer propaganda."

Now Mrs. Wompers reached behind the glass counter and held a fistful of brochures in her hand. I recognized them from the Welcome Wagon meeting yesterday morning. They were printed on spring green paper and explained about something called Concerned Americans for Rational Energy, or CARE. Mrs. Wompers had attempted to pass them out to the other women and explain what CARE was about. The eyes of the other women had glazed over; at the end of the meeting, they had left most of the brochures behind.

Mrs. Wompers said, "We're meeting with the school counselor soon. On Tuesday, isn't it, Harry? I'm sure everything can be straightened out."

"So," said Mr. Wompers to me, "let's tell you about our plans."

All three of them explained. They would keep the trinkets and souvenirs for now. But they seemed most excited about adding the bookstore. They would offer used books for sale or trade, but they intended to acquire books of regional interest: books on the history of the eastern Carolinas, on its vegetation and landscape, on its history and folklore and music.

I remembered what my mother said after Mrs. Wompers had left the Welcome Wagon meeting: "Now, tell me," she had tsked, "what shopper is going to want to stop in to *buy* books when Easton has a perfectly good lending library?"

"We're hoping," Mr. Wompers said, "to encourage reading by our book offerings. Nowadays people get too much of their information from the movies and television."

Suddenly Brenda blurted, "Even so, Dad, people are never going to stop being fascinated by movies and TV. Movies, especially. Tell Gen about Hollywood, Dad." Her face lit up with excitement.

I was eager to hear about Hollywood, but suddenly Mr. Wompers frowned, and the shop fell silent. Running his pale hands over his bald scalp, he said, "Later, Brenda. We've got to concern ourselves with this shop for now. We can reminisce with this young woman about Hollywood some other time."

I forgot all about Hollywood. I had never heard any adult refer to me as a "young woman" before.

11

found myself at the Womperses' house, which was several miles from mine, less than a week later. It was on the other side of Easton. I was there because of Algebra I.

On Monday, Mr. Latham, my Algebra I teacher, had peered out from under his bushy eyebrows. "I was certain that your low score on the diagnostic test was some kind of mistake," he offered. "In fact, I looked over your transcript, and you're a smart girl, Genevieve."

With a sharpened pencil Mr. Latham now pointed to the D on my first quiz. "I think we ought to get you a tutor. Nip this problem in the bud."

I'd been hoping I could scuttle from test to test in Algebra I, hiding out like a hermit crab among scores of Cs with the occasional B for camouflage. Mr. Latham, apparently, was rejecting that strategy.

The tutor he assigned was Brenda Wompers.

My mother would have been appalled at the condition of the Womperses' house. Stacks of magazines and books were scattered about parts of the living room. Newspapers with mastheads I had never heard of sprawled on table-tops like vacationers on beaches. Day-old supper plates and abandoned coffee cups occupied empty pockets of the room. Damaged boxes, filled with Hawaiian leis or wooden back scratchers for the souvenir shop, were stacked in corners. A pair of reading glasses was draped over a torn lampshade faded to the color of old photographs. At my house, books took their proper places on bookshelves, newspapers were folded neatly and discarded every Friday, dishes and cups went immediately to the kitchen counter, damaged goods were placed in the garage, and every pair of glasses had its assigned leather case. Still, something inside me reveled in the disarray that was the Womperses' house.

In Brenda's bedroom, we bent over the textbook pages swimming with x's and y's and exponents and equal signs.

As I tried to concentrate I couldn't help but notice the contents of Brenda's room. A huge aquarium filled with exotic-looking fish bubbled and hummed on the far wall. A bookshelf was strewn with gadgets and tools that reminded me of my father's *Popular Mechanics* projects. Brenda explained that the old leather boots mounted on springs were her attempt to design pogo shoes that would work like Pogo sticks, minus, of course, those unwieldy sticks. She held up a gadget that consisted of a parachute device mounted on some rotors and screws that she was trying to turn into an air-propelled watercraft.

Brenda's room wasn't like any room I'd ever seen before. Certainly it was nothing like the room in which I had spent hours with Sally Redmond. Sally's room had had a white canopy bed with a pink organdy spread and matching window curtains. A pink rug had adorned the floor, and stuffed animals had been stacked up in a neat pyramid in one corner. We'd spent hours before Sally's pink and white dressing table and mirror set applying makeup and lipstick which we were forbidden to wear outside the house.

Although I was distracted by the hodgepodge of books, posters, boxes, equipment, and strewn clothing in the room, Brenda's enthusiasm helped keep me focused.

"It's about getting one side to match up with the other," Brenda exclaimed. "What's on the left side of the equation needs to equal what's on the right side of the equation, see?"

I didn't see, but I didn't say so. Eventually I got the hang of how you switched things from one side of the equation to the other, but the effort reminded me of one of those trick wallets you purchased at the carnival, flipping the sections from side to side to hide the dollar bill. I wondered why you'd want to resort to such trickery in the first place.

"I love math," Brenda announced. "It's like solving a giant puzzle. Math makes sense," she gushed.

I didn't say what I was thinking—that math seemed the most senseless activity ever invented.

"But I like physics even better than math," Brenda added. "Physics *uses* math, of course. But physics explains everything in the world. Why things go up. Why they fall down. How fast a missile will travel. How soon it will stop."

I didn't confess that these mysteries were meaningless to me. I wanted to understand different mysteries: why my father was so obsessive, why my mother was so conventional, how I could pass algebra, how I would survive without Sally Redmond.

Brenda didn't require prodding to go on. "And I think Mr. Reuthven is almost as good a physics teacher as Mr. Isaacs in California. Mr. Reuthven has given us the keenest project. We have to use physics to explain something that seems unexplainable or magical."

I had no idea what she was talking about. Physics all by itself seemed unexplainable enough.

"I'm doing the flying saucer project. I'm sure most of the sightings are just ordinary astronomical objects like planets or stars, don't you?"

I wasn't so sure. My cousin Wills and Gunner had been involved with two of the sightings. The first one Wills and Gunner witnessed occurred when they'd been on the beach at the same time as Walt Gaithers and Ed McCracken.

They'd seen a sparkling sphere winking low on the horizon at sunset. The second occurred when Wills had been out walking Gunner late at night, at the time when Janice Neddeger and Iris Campbell had seen their flying saucer. Wills had insisted to the newspaper reporter that he'd seen nothing unusual that night; besides, Gunner had given no reaction, and he could read that dog better than any book. Janice Neddeger had told the newspaper reporter for the *Easton Eagle* that you couldn't believe the account of a retard.

I saw that Brenda would have talked about physics whether I was in the room or not.

"I have a theory about things," she said. "I told Mr. Reuthven about it."

"Uh-huh," I responded absently, distracted by Brenda's walls. They were covered with book posters with futuristic themes: flaming rockets powering through the blackness of space; eerie creatures spying on earth from the portholes of saucer-shaped ships; silver submarines powered by the atom and diving to the bottom of the sea. Sally had posters on her walls, but they were pictures of movie stars like Marilyn Monroe or James Dean, not pictures from books.

"My theory is that in a time like ours, a time filled with incredible explosions in science, you can expect *more* things that seem unexplainable or magical, not *fewer.*"

I blinked. She had completely lost me.

"I mean, Genevieve, haven't you heard all the silly stuff about UFOs and ESP and Bridey Murphy nowadays?"

"Sure, Brenda," I said. "I've heard about those things." I didn't confess that they didn't seem altogether "silly" to me.

"Well, Gen," Brenda went on, "when science is giving you nuclear reactors and electron microscopes and particle accelerators, people get scared. It's almost like they have to counteract all the new scientific truths with magical thinking."

I was confused by Brenda's way of thinking about things. Sally and I were never as serious as Brenda.

I steadied myself by studying the walls again. My eyes landed on a long list written in Brenda's own bold hand. The title at the top of the list read, "Rules for Thinking." I read hurriedly through the list:

> *An idea is not necessarily true because you would like to believe it.*
> *An idea is not necessarily false because you would hate to believe it.*
> *An idea is not necessarily true or false because your parents, friends, or a person of high status believes it.*

Now Brenda moved across the room to pull clothes out of boxes. "Want to try on some things?" she asked. "Mother lets me go through the donations before we put them in the thrift section of the store."

I watched as Brenda held up a series of items: a pair of hand-knit purple and green socks, a yellow rain slicker, a paisley vest, a black beret.

"Here, Gen," she said. "You pick out what you want."

I was more comfortable diving into the boxes of clothes. Sally and I had spent hours before her mirror swirling our felt circle skirts or folding our bobby socks to just the right length.

I giggled as I held up a pink and brown striped blouse. It was different from the current style of a demure blouse with a Peter Pan collar, a meek-looking flat collar with rounded ends that met in the front and reminded you that you weren't yet grown up. This blouse, on the other hand, was made of a silky synthetic material and had a plunging neckline. It reminded me of a picture in one of my mother's magazines of Marilyn Monroe in white chiffon, with a gust from the sidewalk grille blowing her skirt naughtily upward. As I slipped the slinky blouse over my head, I liked the way it clung to my body, soft as a second skin.

"That looks terrific," Brenda said.

I had to admit I liked the way it felt. I wasn't so sure about how it looked.

"You should wear lively things like that, Gen. Things that are cheerful. Your face always looks so serious. As if your life's been full of tragedies."

I did not respond. *No*, I thought, *just full of my father's view of the future.*

Brenda reached across me and lifted a packet of cigarettes from the table beside the mirror. She shook out a cigarette for herself and then tilted the packet in my direction. "Want one?" she asked.

I shook my head as Brenda struck a match. I felt my body flood with fear. My parents would kill me if they ever thought I took even a single drag.

I watched Brenda inhale. Her cigarette smoking was different from that of the other girls. Janice, April, Renee, and Iris coughed and sputtered when they smoked behind their parents' backs; Brenda smoked with the experience of someone who smoked all the time.

I waved away the smoke as Brenda went through another box and picked up a few items of jewelry. Then before I could protest, she clamped the cigarette between her teeth while she held some gold earrings to my face and draped a jangly necklace around my neck. I frowned at the earrings, but I liked the way the necklace jingled when I moved.

Now I watched Brenda button up the paisley vest and slip the black beret on her head. The outfit seemed right on her. The paisley shapes wiggled like the pictures of the paramecia in my biology textbook. I especially liked the beret. Angled atop her head, the beret pressed down over

Brenda's curls, restraining the enthusiasm of the ringlets that bobbled atop her head whenever she talked. The cigarette dangling from her lips made her look like a jaded poet in a café.

"We've got to wear these outfits tomorrow," Brenda exclaimed.

"*To school*?" I was horrified.

"Take them home," she said. "Think about it."

I wrapped the necklace up in the blouse. "OK," I said. "I'll think about it."

As Brenda reached across the mirror to stub out her cigarette she tripped on a pile of books lying on the floor. I glanced at a score of titles: *The Martian Chronicles*; *Brave New World*; *I, Robot*.

"You want to borrow something else?" She was indicating the books now, not the clothes.

I was astonished by the question. Sally and I read magazines, not books. But I could remember how much I had loved reading books as a child.

"My parents let me go through the used books before we shelve them in the store. They say young people need to read all they can. It prepares them for the adult years. Sort of like squirrels storing up nuts for the winter." Brenda smiled broadly.

"Here," she said, picking up a worn paperback from the floor. I read the title: *Catcher in the Rye*. "You might like this. I finished it just before we left California. I stayed up all night reading it," she added proudly.

I was astonished. "You mean your parents *let* you stay up all night?" My parents would never have permitted me to stay up all night. For any kind of reason whatsoever.

"Sure," she said. "And Mother let me skip the first two periods of school the next morning so I could catch up on my sleep."

I couldn't believe what Brenda said. Had her parents really *encouraged* her to skip school?

"At the moment," Brenda continued, "*Catcher in the Rye* is my favorite book because it uses my favorite word."

I wrinkled my brow. "Favorite *word*?"

"Uh-huh," Brenda nodded, passing the book to me. "*Pervert*. Holden Caufield, the main character, uses it over and over again. *Pervert*. Isn't that a great word?"

"Hmmmm," I said. I was not familiar with that word, but I was afraid of showing my ignorance. I kept silent.

"You know," said Brenda, turning to me to explain, "if Janice Neddeger wears a pink blouse, then April Summers has to wear a pink blouse."

I nodded.

"That makes them both 'perverts,'" said Brenda. "And if Janice Neddeger subscribes to *Seventeen*—"

"Then Carol Calloway subscribes to *Seventeen*," I replied.

"Perverts," said Brenda.

"Perverts," I mimicked her.

Then I began to laugh. I felt something heavy lift and inflate on our laughter; after the heaviness ascended, I felt almost as light as I did when I floated in the ocean.

Now my eyes fell on a different book lying on the floor. It was a book I had loved as a child. Instinctively, my hand reached out for the bright red cover.

As I reached for it, I saw Brenda frown. "How did that book get in here? It's meant for the children's rack."

She must have seen the look on my face that said I had once loved this children's story, *The Story of Ferdinand.* In the summertime I brought stacks of books home from the library. But when I reached junior high, my father had declared most of the books that interested me off-limits, and I had lost interest in reading.

"You can take it if you'd like," Brenda added generously.

"Thanks," I said. "My aunt Minna used to read this book to me."

"Sure," Brenda said.

"Well, I'd better be going," I said. "Thanks for the help with the algebra."

I gathered up my things: algebra book, spiral notepad, pencils, two borrowed books, a blouse, and a necklace. As I stood at the doorway to say good-bye it struck me that I had arrived like an empty suitcase and left with it filled to overflowing.

12

I supposed eating with Brenda Wompers was better than eating alone.

But I wasn't completely sure.

I was uncomfortable with the way Brenda bounded up to me as I ate my egg salad sandwich and the sideways glances thrown at Brenda and me from the adjoining tables.

Brenda sat down without asking. She was wearing the black beret and the paisley vest. "Have you figured out the difference between binomials and polynomials?" she asked bluntly.

"I tried to," I said.

Brenda looked pleased. "Good," she said, applauding my ignorance. "Then I'm in no danger of losing my job."

Brenda chomped on a carrot stick pulled from the pocket of her skirt. No one had chopped and cut it into tiny sticks to fit into a Tupperware compartment.

"Is that all you're having for lunch?"

Brenda looked absently at the long orange stick. "Sure, why?"

The carrot looked as if it had been pulled straight from the garden. A few smudges of dirt still clung to its sides. I reached over to flick them off. "It needs washing," I said. "I'll take it over to the water fountain for you," I offered.

"No, thanks," Brenda said. "The dirt's actually good for you. It has a lot of nutrients. My parents and I don't believe in processed food. The more you process it, the less healthy it is for you. Raw food's best."

I felt even more uneasy: I was sitting beside someone who liked to eat dirt.

Now, as Brenda often did, she suddenly pulled a new topic out of thin air. "Is there a weather station nearby?" she asked.

I looked back at Brenda. The razor-straight glasses gave her a serious air, but the tight black ringlets above them made her look comical.

"Sure," I said. "The weather station monitors all our hurricanes."

"Ah-*ha*! I *thought* so!" she exulted. She looked as gleeful as a pirate stumbling onto a treasure chest. "That explains one of those flying saucer sightings. The one that was said to be a reddish-colored glowing saucer disk."

"Oh," I said. That wasn't one Wills and Gunner had seen. I wasn't as familiar with that sighting.

"Oh, it's so *logical*! So *consistent*!" exclaimed Brenda, throwing back her head. "All over the country weather balloons have been mistaken for flying saucers. Especially late in the afternoon or at sunset."

I fiddled with my celery stick as I listened, turning the stick upside down. From that angle, with the leaves on the bottom and the shoot firing upward, it reminded me of the rocket ships in my *Weekly Reader* that scientists were building in hopes of reaching the moon.

Now Brenda grabbed my hand, and the celery stick shook. "Tell me, Gen," she said urgently. "Tell me—in detail—about that sighting by Janice Neddeger and Iris Campbell."

"Well,"—I shrugged—"I don't think I know much more about it than everyone else knows."

Brenda hauled her rucksack onto the lunch table and began rooting around in it. "But you're careful with words," she said, digging like a mole. "You've got an eye for detail. I can trust what you say."

I felt a tiny bird fluttering inside, ruffling wings of pride. "Well, I'll try, Brenda," I said.

She had finally found the pencil and paper she'd been looking for. "I want to take this down exactly."

"OK," I said. "It was late on a Friday night. In April. Near the end of the month. The last weekend in April, I think."

Brenda sat forward in her hard plastic chair, listening.

"They were on Easton Boulevard. You know, that's the street that runs right along the beach."

Brenda nodded, gripping the pencil and writing carefully. "What time?"

"Maybe around midnight. Apparently Janice had taken her parents' new car out without their permission. Her parents had gone to bed early or something. But they'd just bought that beautiful Ford Fairlane convertible."

I ran my fingers up and down the celery stalk, trying to remember everything I knew. "Iris Campbell was with her," I added. "And Wills said Brad Connors had been with them, too. Only Brad ran away from the scene and denies ever being there."

Brenda's eyes lurched like tire wheels suddenly braked. "*Wills* was there? Your *cousin*?"

"Uh-huh," I nodded. "He was the first one on the scene. He'd been out walking Gunner and some of the other animals at Petty's Pets. Wills was the one who ran off to call the ambulance and everything."

"How terrible was the wreck?"

"Awful," I remembered. "The car was wrapped around a telephone pole."

"And how did the flying saucer explanation come about?"

"Well, Janice and Iris said they'd suddenly seen this weird saucer-shaped object hovering over the beach, and Iris had a camera. She always does. Photography's her hobby."

Brenda nodded, encouraging me to go on.

"They had been driving around trying to take pictures of the UFO. They said the saucer had portholes all around the sides and made a whirring noise like a vacuum cleaner. They said chasing the saucer was what caused them to wreck."

"And what did Wills say?"

"Wills didn't see a thing. Didn't hear any whirring noise, either. And none of the animals made a sound. Animals tend to notice things. They're sensitive to changes in the atmosphere. All Wills heard was the sound of the crash and the breaking glass and all."

"But there were pictures."

Now Brenda ruffled in her rucksack again and brought out the newspaper clippings. "I'm not sure I can explain it yet," she said, her eyebrows moving together beneath the rims of her glasses. "It's the only sighting I can't quite account for."

Brenda had obviously been studying those photographs. There were all kinds of arrows and squiggles marked on the photographs of last April's *Easton Eagle*.

"And this article," Brenda went on, "mentions the account of a Lucas William. That must be Wills, right?"

I nodded.

"But it only mentions Wills's account in a phrase or two. Why is that?"

I looked down into the separate compartments of my Tupperware lunch box. The compartments kept the egg salad away from the celery and the orange slices. I wished I could sort out my feelings about Wills just as neatly.

I recalled those painful memories of Wills with the other boys.

Link Palmer would tease him. "I hear you're a retard, Wills," he would say.

"Am not," Wills would answer.

"You are so," Link would say.

"Not," Wills would reply.

Then Brad Connors would join in. "Well, Wills, if you're not a retard, then you're just plain stupid."

I looked over at Brenda. Her eyes were still curious.

I sighed. Wills had told it all to me. He'd worn that sad look that melted his face when he realized people were calling him names. "Janice had told the reporter not to believe Wills. That he couldn't be believed. Because he was a 'retard.'"

Brenda got very quiet. "Oh," was all she said.

I could feel the tears beginning to sting. I chomped hard on my celery stick, willing the tears back into my eye sockets. "Why," I asked Brenda Wompers, "does Janice Neddeger act like that?"

Brenda paused a minute, thinking. "Have you heard the story of the scorpion and the frog?"

Again, Brenda had thrown me off course with an abrupt change of topic. "The *scorpion*? And the *frog*?" I asked.

Brenda nodded. "See, there's this scorpion," she said. She was flipping her pencil restlessly. "It needs a ride across the river, see. So it hitches a ride across the river on the frog's back. Halfway across the river, the scorpion stings the frog." Then she jabbed the point of her pencil into the tabletop for emphasis.

"Why?" I asked. I had stopped chewing on the hard shreds of celery in my mouth.

"That's just the question the *frog* wants answered. It's like you just asked a moment ago: 'Why does Janice act like that?'"

I was very quiet. I wanted desperately to know the answer.

"The scorpion answered the frog," Brenda announced, "very matter-of-factly."

"What did he say?" I could feel my teeth grinding at the tough stalk of celery again.

"'It's in my nature,' the scorpion admitted."

I swallowed.

Then Brenda was suddenly back to the flying saucer subject again. "Was the top up or down?"

"What?"

"The top. The top of the Fairlane convertible. Was it up or down?"

"Well, I don't know," I said, struggling to follow her. "I guess it was up."

I saw the question marks in Brenda's eyes.

"Well, Janice's and Iris's injuries weren't too serious," I explained. "If the top had been down, their injuries would have been far worse. They could have died."

Brenda nodded. She was scribbling furiously on her paper.

"Why?" I asked.

Now Brenda looked up from her scribbling. "So how'd they get such good pictures?"

"What?" I wasn't following her.

"How'd they get such good pictures of the UFO if the top was up?"

I shrugged.

Now Brenda suddenly banged on the lunch table, startling me the way she had when she had banged on the aluminum heating ducts in the basement during the Civil Defense drill. "Hey," she said, "did you get started on *Catcher in the Rye*?"

I nodded, attempting to move on to yet another new topic.

Last night I had gone to bed with my dictionary and the books Brenda had given me. I started with the dictionary.

My finger scanned the runway of words and landed. "*Pervert*," I read. "Noun. A perverted person, especially one who practices sexual deviations." I was confused. Sexual deviations, I thought, had something to do with the peep shows on the darkest section of the carnival grounds or the traffic in ladies in cheap purple dresses on the west side of town. I thought perhaps Brenda had simply misinterpreted the word's meaning. Still, I wondered, *Shouldn't you be completely sure about what words mean before you use them?*

"How're you liking the book?" Brenda asked.

"It's great," I lied. I didn't tell her that I had been bored with it. Holden Caufield wasn't anything like me. I suppose we were both unhappy, but he was bitterly so, and arrogant and apathetic at the same time. Still, I pressed on through the story.

I hadn't run across the word *pervert* even once, but I had read the word *phony* several times now. I wondered, isn't *phony* a better word to describe the other girls than *pervert*?

I also didn't tell Brenda that as I grew bored, I reached for the other book she had loaned me.

When I was young, I would beg Aunt Minna to read it over and over again whenever she visited. My parents never seemed to have time to read to me.

I remembered the feel of Aunt Minna beside me like something warm pulled from the oven as we scanned the pen-and-ink drawings of young Ferdinand the bull, quietly sitting under the cork tree and smelling the flowers.

"What kind of story is that?" my father had demanded, looking up from his newspaper.

"It's just a *story*, George," Minna had said. "Go back to your newspaper."

When Minna had finished reading about the bull who preferred smelling flowers to fighting in the bullfights, my father had put down his newspaper again.

"That's a terrible story," he had declared. "The world is a tough place. Children need to learn how to *fight*, not *run away*."

"Yes, the world *can* be a tough place, George. So why can't we just let children be children for as long as we can?" Minna had smiled at me.

"No wonder Wills is spoiled," my father had harrumphed.

"*Loved*, George," Minna had said.

Somehow, after that, I never asked Aunt Minna to read this story again.

Snapping back to the present, I suddenly noticed a group of girls at another table. They were giggling and pointing at Brenda and me. I wondered what they were laughing about, and then I realized that Brenda was wearing the paisley vest and the black beret. I gave a cowardly sigh of relief that I hadn't worn the silky pink and brown striped blouse. Brenda got up and marched over to the girls. I slunk down in my seat. She stood in front of them, looking like Bugs Bunny in a beret. She pointed the gnawed end of her carrot stick at them and asked, "Why don't you act like *women* instead of *girls*?"

As Brenda turned around, the girls stared awkwardly at their plates, astonished at being confronted so directly.

As I watched Brenda strutting away, I thought of my mother's magazines. They were kept on the coffee table, their covers spread out across the polished surface in the shape of a fan. Inside were pictures of dramatic things taking place in the world outside of Easton: Willie Mays sliding into first; Jerry Lee Lewis shaking his body and plunking piano keys; a dark-skinned Mr. Brown on the steps of the Supreme Court building, beaming over the decision that his daughter could not be denied admission to an all-white elementary school.

Brenda reminded me of the people in those pictures. Around her something was always *happening*.

13

had been allowed to stay for supper with the Womperses on Tuesday night after my algebra tutoring. Brenda and I and Mr. and Mrs. Wompers sat on mismatched chairs at a rickety card table without tablecloths or cloth napkins. Mrs. Wompers was wearing her pink bathrobe and slippers. Mr. Wompers was wearing a moth-eaten blue sweater.

Supper consisted of pancakes, which Mr. and Mrs. Wompers took turns scraping indifferently from the electric skillet. We lavished the pancakes with streams of maple syrup as thick as cough medicine. It felt like a picnic.

After supper Mr. and Mrs. Wompers and Brenda and I played a game at the same rickety card table. My family didn't play games together. Occasionally my mother played solitaire while my father read the newspaper. Scrabble was a game I had never played before.

"You work well with words," Mr. Wompers said after I

finished making the five-letter word *whale*. Placing the *w* on a double letter square earned me eight points.

"Tell Gen about Hollywood," Brenda suggested. "Tell her about your collection of films, Dad. The ones you brought with you from Hollywood." Then she made the word *elbow* off of the *w* in my *whale* and grinned with glee.

But Mr. Wompers changed the subject to politics. "Your parents are both Republicans," he announced.

"How did you know that?" I asked.

"Because most of America's Republican nowdays," he said, consulting the instruction book about whether he could put a foreign word down on the board, "'I like Ike' and all that. Blind approbation. Trish and I, we were Stevenson voters."

In the last presidential election General Dwight D. "Ike" Eisenhower had easily defeated Adlai Stevenson. I had never heard of a single person who had voted for Stevenson. No one could resist Ike's broad smile and grandfatherly demeanor. Stevenson, from what I could tell, was too concerned, too thoughtful-looking. He seemed more like a professor than a president. In fact, he reminded me of Mr. Wompers.

"Trish and I think Ike prefers golfing to governing," Mr. Wompers said.

Now Mrs. Wompers's lively, kittenish face frowned. "I've no respect for the man," she muttered, reaching across the Scrabble board and patting her husband's hand while her daughter made the word *paste*. "Eisenhower hasn't stood up to the witch hunts that have been going on for too many years."

I wondered at Mrs. Wompers's term: *witch hunts*. My father used the same term to describe the efforts to bring Senator McCarthy down. Mrs. Pagano had used the term to describe the events in Salem, Massachusetts, in our unit on colonial history.

"Our great president," said Mr. Wompers, twisting his lips into a sarcastic smile, "stood by and let Senator Mc-Carthy feed us all this Cold War hysteria. Let McCarthy accuse innocent people of being Communists. Folks in the State Department. Folks in the army."

"Folks in Hollywood, too, Dad," Brenda chimed in.

"Thank goodness," Mrs. Wompers sighed, "McCarthy's finally been revealed to be the liar he is." She swept back the wave of gray hair that had fallen over her eye and exchanged four of her letter squares. "He's finished."

I thought about the conversations that had taken place at my house. Senator McCarthy had been discredited and would likely be censured, but I also knew that my father still supported McCarthy.

Turning to me and changing the subject, Mrs. Wompers asked, "What do *you* think of the Civil Defense program up at your school, Genevieve?"

I mumbled, "I feel like it's pretty scary."

"But what do you *think*?" Mrs. Wompers said, not unkindly but earnestly.

I wasn't sure I had much of an opinion to offer.

"Well, Harry and I are quite unhappy with the program," Mrs. Wompers said, making the word *captive* on the Scrabble board. "That school wouldn't even let me put my brochures out on the desk alongside the government's propaganda. What bothers me most about it are all the inaccuracies they feed you young people as if they were bona fide facts."

Mrs. Wompers was almost out of letters, but she was entirely unaware that she was about to go out of the game.

"That program up at your school makes it sound like nuclear attacks are survivable," added Mr. Wompers.

I winced. "*Your* school." As if it were *my* fault.

"There's no mention of the kind of life that people would lead even if they *did* survive it," said Mrs. Wompers.

Now Mrs. Wompers lit a cigarette and pulled a folded, coffee-stained paper from the pocket of her housecoat. She unfolded it carefully and passed it to me.

The paper read:

The undersigned hereby petition the school board to permit supplemental information about the consequences of nuclear war to be presented as part of the ninth-grade Civil Defense curriculum at Easton High School. The accuracy of such information is to be

validated by the latest scientific research. The information is not intended to supplant but to serve as a correction to the information currently being presented.

As I studied the words I wondered, first of all, if anyone else in Easton would ever consider signing it. Sec-
ondly, looking at the challenging words like *supplant* and
validated, I wondered if anyone in Easton would *understand* it.

"We'd like you to sign it, Genevieve," Mr. Wompers
said softly. "You know a lot of people in Easton. Your family's lived here a long time. If we can get a few local folks
to align with us, we should be able to make these needed
changes."

I didn't know what to say. I knew my parents wouldn't
want me to sign such a thing; I knew how strongly my father favored the Civil Defense program. On the other
hand, the petition seemed to be asking only that additional information, information that was accurate, be allowed to be presented. It wasn't suggesting that the
program be abolished. Still, I didn't know how to answer
the plea in Mr. Wompers's eyes.

Brenda saved me. "Gen's not like a lot of people in
Easton. She doesn't rush into things. She likes to take her
time to think. I doubt she's ready to sign right away. But
maybe eventually. Right, Gen?"

I swallowed hard. "Maybe so," I muttered.

"We have an appointment to meet with your principal tomorrow morning," Mrs. Wompers announced.

Mr. and Mrs. Wompers and Brenda all nodded their heads while I felt the sting of *your principal.* All three of them had forgotten about the Scrabble game.

"Genevieve," asked Brenda's father, "have you ever read *Hiroshima*?" He picked up a dog-eared book atop a stack of newspapers.

I shook my head.

"You should," Mr. Wompers declared.

"It describes the bomb blast," added his wife.

He handed the book to me. It tingled in my fingers. As if even its cover might be radioactive.

"Yes," said Brenda. "The Japanese with their eyebrows burned off. The vomiting. The skin sliding from their faces and hands."

I shuddered.

"Did you know that the women had burn patterns on their bodies in the shapes of the flowers on their kimonos?"

I began to think of all the times Brenda had volunteered shocking comments in class. Sometimes I wondered if perhaps she was as interested in arousing as in informing.

I shuddered. "How do you know all of this?"

"My mother," Brenda added. "She volunteered for CARE in California. CARE is an antinuclear peace group."

"That my wife founded," Mr. Wompers added proudly.

Now Brenda reached across the table and shook a cigarette from her mother's package of Chesterfields. As Brenda inhaled on her cigarette, she suddenly looked much older. I watched her blow cigarette smoke across the Scrabble board.

"I can see what you're thinking, Genevieve," Mr. Wompers said, addressing me with his thin, bemused smile. "It's written all over your face. You're shocked that Trish and I permit Brenda to smoke."

I coughed on the plume of smoke that drifted under my nose. But I said nothing.

"Harry and I had a good talk about it," Mrs. Wompers said. "And then with Brenda, of course." She ran her plump hand through her silver hair. "We just don't find it reasonable to deny our daughter what we don't deny ourselves," she offered, lighting another cigarette of her own.

"It seemed hypocritical," concluded Mr. Wompers, his brows knitted thoughtfully.

I pressed my fingers together, preparing to rise from the table to review one more time for the algebra test I'd be taking tomorrow. I could still feel the sticky pancake syrup on my fingertips. I looked around in vain for a napkin.

14

"You mean there's another storm on the way, Dad?"

It was hard to imagine *two* hurricanes in one season, but my father had spread his hurricane map out across the dining room table once more. Green, yellow, and red flags marched past the Bahamas and curved toward Easton in a northwesterly direction. The line of flags stopped at a point very near where Hurricane Carol had formed less than two weeks ago.

"Um-hmm," he muttered. "Hurricanes. They're as erratic as women. They're calling this one Edna," he said.

Selfishly, I worried about the pool. Since Hurricane Carol, Uncle Bud and my father had spent late evenings working either on Uncle Bud's roof or my father's pool project. Uncle Bud and my father even sometimes worked in the dark under floodlights.

Of course, I didn't dare show my excitement over the progress. But as I saw where they intended for an earthmover to clear a large swath of dirt and for an excavating machine to dig a big hole, I felt my own heart thump. It was approaching mid-September. A pool was still possible by late fall.

But I not only worried about the storm and its effect on our pool, I worried about the storm and the Wompers family. They were still in the middle of setting up shop, and they understood even less about hurricanes than they did about shopkeeping.

I was even more worried about the Womperses' meeting with Mr. Wrinkle on Wednesday morning. The school was in an uproar. Our principal had denied their requests. I was fairly certain that Mr. and Mrs. Wompers had merely asked to have their petition posted. But people were saying that Mr. Wompers and our principal had thrown fists and that the police led the Womperses away in handcuffs. It was said Mr. and Mrs. Wompers were threatening to hire a lawyer and sue the school. I knew these rumors were unfounded: Mr. Wompers wouldn't know how to throw his fists at anyone, and the Womperses could hardly afford a lawyer.

The school had been swamped with phone calls, and the *Easton Eagle* reporter-photographer had begun roaming the halls, taking down student reactions and snapping photographs. The superintendent of schools had granted Mr. and Mrs. Wompers an emergency hearing before the school board on Thursday night.

But then on Thursday the weather bureau announced

the approach of Hurricane Edna, and the emergency hearing had to be postponed.

"So what's it like to be in a hurricane?" Mrs. Wompers asked that afternoon when I appeared with Wills and Gunner in tow at the front of their shop.

"Scary," I confessed. "The power goes out, and the wind rips at the roof. You can hear trees and utility poles swaying and snapping. And you have to be careful even after it's over. Hot power lines are lying all over the place." I looked down and saw that Mrs. Wompers and Brenda had been working in their bare feet. "You don't dare go barefoot," I warned.

Mrs. Wompers reached for her sandals, but Brenda wiggled her toes playfully in response.

Wills was a big help. He drove the nails while I held the plywood boards across the Womperses' store windows. Gunner padded about, lifting his head and sniffing the air on the boardwalk. Long John Silver and Midnight jumped about, enjoying the activity. When we finished nailing, Mr. Wompers said, "But the ocean looks so *calm* now."

Even though the surface of the sea was still quiet, I could read the signs that meant an approaching storm: the falling temperature, the tiny gusts of wind, the slant of the sea grass across the shoreline. "Looks can be deceiving," I replied.

Over the years I had learned a lot from my father and from the hurricane precaution lessons at school. A hurricane can stretch six hundred miles in diameter and reach eight miles into the air; *urican* was a Caribbean Indian word that meant "big wind"; last year was the first season in which hurricanes were named for women.

"My father's kind of a hurricane nut. He gets out his maps and his shortwave radio at the first sign of a storm. Stays up to date on every twist and turn. He keeps a list with each storm name and the category it falls in."

"Category?" asked Mr. Wompers.

"Yes. Hurricanes are rated in categories from one to five. A Cat One is a storm with winds over seventy-four miles an hour. A Cat Five has winds over one hundred fifty-five miles an hour."

Brenda was scratching her head, thinking out loud. "How do they measure the winds?"

I shrugged my shoulders. "I don't know. I guess the weather station's got all kinds of measuring stuff."

Brenda wasn't really listening. She was talking to herself. "I'm sure it's some kind of anemometer. But it's got to be a really special one to measure winds that high. I'm wondering if Mr. Reuthven knows what they use." Then her face lit up like a struck match. "I know! I'll try to build my *own* anemometer. It can't require much more than a rotating pole with some kind of measuring gauge."

Mr. and Mrs. Wompers beamed at their daughter.

"Let us know if you need any help with it," Mr. Wompers said.

Brenda was rooting through boxes and cartons, not wasting any time.

Now Mrs. Wompers turned to me. "What kind of category was Hurricane Carol in?" she asked.

"A Category Two. Pretty mild, as hurricanes go. Even though the winds near Cape Hatteras reached nearly one hundred miles an hour, my dad said the storm surge wasn't so bad."

Brenda held an aluminum rod in her hand and stopped digging to ask, "What's a storm surge?"

"It's a wall of water," I said, glad to offer information to people who seemed to know so much about so many things. "It can reach forty feet. When hurricanes kill people or destroy property, it's either through wind, rain, tornadoes, or storm surge. Most of the people who are killed by a hurricane are killed by the storm surge."

"It reminds me of those Hollywood movies your friends used to work on, Dad," Brenda offered. "You know, the ones with the big scaly monsters rising out of the sea, all the people thrashing about and drowning."

Mr. Wompers nodded, pursed his lips, then turned away to fiddle with some plastic sheets he was using to cover his merchandise.

"You're right, Brenda," I confirmed. "A big monster. A storm surge is exactly like that."

"I'm wondering," she said, "what causes it."

"What causes *what*?" I asked.

"The storm surge." There was a flicker of impatience in her voice.

I stared at Brenda Wompers. She fired off a barrage of questions: Was the surging caused by the wind? A lack of resistance? An abundance of it? Or some combination of many factors?

Now Brenda bent her head into the boxes again. She held up a battered and rusty gauge and laid it next to the aluminum rod.

Now that the windows had been boarded up with plywood, I had to convince the Womperses to get everything up off the floor of the shop.

"You wouldn't believe the power of water," I said, and Wills nodded. "It has a way of seeping into the cracks plugged up against it." I didn't say what I was thinking: The power of water was like the power of rumor, able to destroy every barrier erected against it. You needed to be prepared.

As we fashioned makeshift pallets out of boards laid across bricks, we then heaved bins of souvenirs and cartons of clothes up on them. Gunner rolled around on the floor of the shop and chased his tail. The parrot squawked, "Top o' the mornin'. Good *day.*" The black cat contributed to the merriment by batting at a loose plastic sheet with his paw.

After we had finished, Brenda and her mother and father stared in disbelief at the shop that had now been completely rearranged.

"Whew! That's enough work for one day," Mrs. Wompers said.

"Yes," Mr. Wompers agreed. "Let's send these three young people off for the reward of an ice-cream cone." He reached quickly into his pocket and tossed a handful of quarters to us. "Treat yourselves."

The Sweet Shop was just a few stores down the boardwalk. A bell tinkled as we stepped inside. Brad Connors worked behind the counter, looking silly with that paper hat on his head. He held the metal scoop aloft as we gave our orders. I asked for a cone of strawberry; Brenda asked for a cone of orange sherbet.

When it was Wills's turn, he said, "I'll take a scoop of ribbon fudge."

"It's fudge *ribbon*, Wonderboy," Brad snorted.

Brenda piped up, "And what makes *you* such a genius, Superman?"

I scowled at Brad as the bell tinkled behind us.

The late afternoon was fading into evening, and the sun was trumpeting one long, last blast of heat.

The three of us and Gunner strolled along the boardwalk together. The striped awnings were casting longer shadows; the crowds were beginning to thin. Both Brenda and I were half finished with our ice cream.

"Let's cross to the beach," I said. "Gunner loves the beach."

After we crossed, dodging cars like vacationers, Brenda stopped for a moment outside a wooden cabana shelter. Cabanas dotted the edge of the beach. They looked like miniature canvas circus tents. They contained wooden benches for changing into suits and showers for washing off salt and sand.

Now Brenda bent to pet Gunner, but the dog shyly ducked.

"Gunner doesn't cotton much to strangers," Wills said.

Brenda wasn't easily discouraged. Slowly she extended what was left of her cone of orange sherbet. She watched as Gunner sniffed at the cone and then gingerly poked at it with his nose. When the dog pulled back, startled by the cold, we laughed.

"I was just hoping I might get him to cotton to me." Brenda laughed.

After that we ran along the beach with Gunner, throwing sticks for him retrieve. After a while Wills had to get back to work, but when he left, Gunner allowed not only me but also Brenda to nuzzle him under his chin.

Then I introduced Brenda to the beach that I loved. We ran alongside the green spears of beach grass. We rolled down the gentle dunes. We climbed the line of rugged jetties that stretched into the ocean like a lobster's carapace.

Brenda said, "You know a lot about hurricanes, Genevieve."

I shrugged. "Well, maybe," I said. "But there's not as much to know about hurricanes as there is to know about nuclear bombs."

Now Brenda turned an impish grin on me. "You're plain wrong about that, Gen," she said. "Only three things you need to know about nuclear war. One is to put your hands behind your neck," she said, placing her hands behind her neck. As she did so, the wind ballooned the hem of her skirt. "Two is to put your head between your legs," she said, bending over, putting her head between her legs, and giving herself a view of the more populated end of the beach. From upside down, the black curls on her head bounced like springs. "Three," she added, "is to kiss your butt good-bye!"

The laughter bubbled inside me like syrup simmering on a stove. I hadn't laughed like this since last spring when Sally and I had sat before her pink and white dressing table, applying makeup to look like Lucy Ricardo. We had widened our mouths with slashes of lipstick red as stop signs. We had ringed our eyes with thick fringes of lashes steeped in gobs of mascara. And we had laughed so hard that the tears had streamed from our eyes, smudging the makeup.

15

My family prepared for the storm in our usual way. We brought in the outside furniture and the garbage cans. We boarded the windows with plywood. We bought extra batteries. We filled the bathtub with water. Then we waited.

Reading *Hiroshima,* I had been learning more and more about nuclear disaster. The explosion at Hiroshima had come as a complete surprise, and people had not known to take shelter. Scores of men, women, and children had been caught in the open; the rest were in homes or businesses that were easily destroyed by the sweeping firestorm. I realized that there were two major differences between a hurricane and an atomic explosion: You could prepare for only one of them, and preparation could make a difference.

Aunt Minna and Uncle Bud had decided to leave town in advance of the storm. They were taking Wills to a hospital in Raleigh. They were concerned about the stiffness in Wills's legs. The doctors would be doing some tests.

Everyone in our family knew Aunt Minna and Uncle Bud feared Wills had contracted polio.

"Thanks for helping out with the roof and for keeping an eye on the house while we're gone," Uncle Bud said to my father. "And for keeping Gunner."

My heart leaped up. I hadn't realized that Gunner would be staying with us.

Gunner had been unwilling to get out of Uncle Bud's truck and part with Wills, but when the dog saw me, he jumped down from the seat of the cab.

Wills passed me a box of treats. "These will often work in a pinch," Wills said.

"Thanks, Wills," I said, slipping the box under my arm and noticing how tired Wills looked. "Good luck in Raleigh."

I knelt down to hug the big yellow dog. I buried my nose in his neck. While Bud and Minna and Wills drove away, I whispered the words from the Lord's Prayer on behalf of Wills: ". . . *deliver us from evil.*"

"I'll let Gunner run outside for as long as he can, Mother," I said. "When the storm hits, he may be cooped inside for a long stretch." I remembered what Wills had told me about shy dogs. Exercise was good for them.

The storm began with whips of wind that swirled the leaves into miniature cyclones. Gunner had noticed the changes even before I did. He had suddenly stopped running and stood still to listen, his head cocked, his fur standing up.

"Gen," my mother called from the kitchen door. "Get inside. Right away!"

I watched my mother's eyes widen as the big dog tramped through a mud puddle on the way in, leaving a trail of dirt across the kitchen floor.

Heading for the living room, Gunner cocked his head and listened to the wind. Then he found a corner by the new étagère. The animal turned his back to us and buried his muzzle into the corner. His ears lay back against his head; his body was trembling.

"Go comfort him, Gen," my mother insisted. "He's scared."

"No, Mother," I said. "Wills says it's wrong to comfort a shy dog for acting shy. The comfort's just a reward for him. Wills says you only reward Gunner when he does something brave."

The wind had been followed by rain. It sounded like giant beanbags being thrown against the house. My father had been hurrying my mother and me into the large closet off the entryway when the thunder started.

Suddenly Gunner bolted, his heavy tail knocking over the étagère. Dirt and leaves from the potted fern that sat atop it were now dumped onto the rug. Gunner galloped from wall to wall, leaping onto the plastic-covered couch, jumping onto the coffee table, scattering my mother's fashion magazines across the room.

"Grab him, Genevieve," ordered my mother.

As I chased after him Gunner leaped ahead, crashing into furniture and tables.

My father had grabbed a broom and started beating the dog to subdue him.

"Don't, Dad," I said, "that won't work!"

Then the frightened animal lifted a leg and urinated on the carpet.

"Oh, that *animal*," shouted my mother. "My beautiful *carpet*!" She rushed to the kitchen, returning with towels and ammonia.

When the dog had stopped to urinate, my father had pounced on him and carried him into the bathroom, closing the bathroom door tight behind him.

"Dad," I shouted. "The worst thing you can do to a shy dog is coop him up. It only makes him more afraid."

Thunder crashed all around, and I winced. My mind filled up with energetic -*ing* participles like those in e. e. cummings's poetry: *banging, crashing, thumping, pounding*. Against the drumbeat of thunder, I could hear Gunner flinging himself against the bathroom door.

Then my mother began to wail at the sounds of sloshing water. "George, the dog is in the bathtub! He's flinging water all over! He'll ruin my bathroom!"

My father hustled my mother and me into the walk-in closet. "We don't have time to worry about that now," he insisted.

With the thunder crashing around us, the big dog kept

hurling himself through the water-filled bathtub and then against the bathroom door. We huddled in the closet.

I quietly seethed as my father tuned in his radio to news about the path of the storm and my mother muttered about the path of destruction that had swept through her house.

It soon appeared that Hurricane Edna was passing over Easton with a more gentle hand than Hurricane Carol had. The power stayed on. The phones still worked. The air conditioner hummed.

In the silence between thunderclaps, my parents talked. The rumors swirling at school had circulated through the grocery stores, the boardwalk shops, and the bridge club meetings of Easton. My parents prodded me with questions. Their first questions were indirect.

"Could that have been Mrs. Wompers I saw in the market yesterday buying up bottled water?" My mother pursed her Kewpie doll lips. "With a scarf over her curlers?"

My mother's question held disdain. In her world a lady never left home in curlers, either with a scarf or without.

"I doubt it," I mumbled. "Mrs. Wompers doesn't really fuss with her hair."

I wondered what my mother would have thought of Mrs. Wompers's dinner table attire of pink house slippers accessorizing her pink bathrobe. Mother had a rule about house slippers: They were to be worn only before nine A.M. or after nine P.M.

"But it could have been Mrs. Wompers," I offered. "I know I told Brenda's folks to stock up on water." Then I lamely changed the subject. "People from California don't know the first thing about hurricanes."

"And what about that tutoring you're doing with their daughter?" my father asked.

"Yes, Genevieve," my mother interjected. "Isn't it time you finished working with that girl?"

"But I'm terrible at algebra, Mother. And my grades are going up."

My father's face brightened. My quiz grades had moved from D and D minus to steady Cs.

"Don't they have *other* tutors?" my mother countered.

"I'd lose so much time getting used to another tutor. Besides, another tutor might not be as good as Brenda."

Now they changed the subject.

"Didn't Mr. Womperjawed lose his job in California?"

"Wasn't he unemployed for a long time, sweetie?"

"I don't know," I answered.

"And why can't you associate with some of those girls with more *personality*?"

"You mean like Janice Neddeger?"

"Yes. And Iris Campbell and April Summers. Those girls are *go-getters.*"

I didn't bother to say that Brenda Wompers had "personality," that she, too, was a go-getter. In her own womperjawed way.

"People from California like to cause commotions, don't they, George?"

My father nodded.

"You can expect them to get all riled up about the things their children study in school," continued my mother.

"And they like to get themselves into the newspaper. They like nothing better than an audience for their crack-brained ideas."

"That's right, George. Californians are such negative personalities."

As the storm churned around us, I ached for Gunner thrashing in the bathroom. I knew how the animal must have felt.

16

O
n Sunday afternoon I biked to the beach to survey Edna's aftermath. I ran through patches of flattened sea grass, kicking off my shoes and skipping to the water's edge. Looking across to the fishing pier and shrimp houses, I was relieved to see them still intact.

Sandpipers scooted along the shore, running about on short, thin legs. Seagulls dipped into the ocean for food, struggling to find an easy meal in the churning surf.

I looked back up to the boardwalk and saw a figure waving at me. From a distance the figure looked very small—like a tiny exclamation point turned upside down in the center of a blank page. I realized it was Brenda.

"Edna wasn't very exciting, was she?" Brenda said when she come closer. "Nothing happened to the souvenir shop. And the pier is all in one piece." She sounded disappointed.

"We can be glad of that," I said, genuinely relieved.

"It's good you took all those precautions, Brenda. What about your house?" I asked. "Any damage there?"

"Nope," Brenda said. "Just lost all of our garbage cans."

"Didn't you bring the garbage cans inside?" I distinctly remembered telling the Womperses to bring in their garbage cans.

"We forgot. Dad had bought a shortwave radio, and Mom spent most of the storm helping him figure out how it worked. And of course I was busy with my anemometer. What about you?"

"Everything was fine." I didn't tell her about Gunner's wild behavior.

"Well," Brenda said, "I don't see why a hurricane's such a big deal. It seemed just like a big, windy rainstorm to me."

I felt irritated. "We were just lucky, Brenda. I don't think the folks in New England felt that way."

Edna had merely skirted Cape Hatteras and the North Carolina coast. But my father, reading aloud from the *Easton Eagle,* had reported that the hurricane made landfall over Cape Cod as a Category Three hurricane and that Martha's Vineyard reported a peak wind gust of 120 miles per hour. The newspaper account was estimating at least twenty deaths and $40 million in damage from the storm.

Brenda's face registered a deep disappointment. "Worst of all was my anemometer."

"Your anemometer?"

Brenda looked stricken, like a child on Christmas morning without a single toy. "I couldn't get the gauge to record the speeds accurately."

"Here, Brenda," I offered, hoping to lighten her mood. "How'd you like to see my secret place?"

"Is it really a *secret*?"

"Well, sort of. Wills knows where it is, of course."

Brenda seemed to welcome the distraction as we hiked up the beach.

Except for a few loose side rails and a single floorboard that had wiggled loose, the lifeguard stand still seemed remarkably sturdy.

"Wow," said Brenda. "This place is really neat. What do you do here?"

I kept quiet. I wasn't sure I could tell Brenda that I often came here to write. But Brenda seemed to understand those things on her own. "I'll bet you do your best writing here," she said.

"I wouldn't call it my best writing necessarily," I said. "I don't always like the result of what I write. Maybe it's sort of like your anemometer. There's a lot of experimenting that goes on to get it right."

Brenda nodded. "I bet I could do some of my own best experimenting here, too."

"Experimenting?"

"You know. With my anemometers and my gauges. I could set them up here. This is a great place for wind experiments. It's up high and out in the open and isolated and all. I'll bet we could do some great experimenting here together. You with your writing, me with my physics."

Did I really want to share this special place with Brenda Wompers, a girl who was only an almost-friend, not a full-fledged one like Sally Redmond?

"But I know you'll have to think about it," she said, as if reading my mind. "Gen Hardcastle's not one to make snap decisions." Then she grinned.

My heart bubbled over with gratitude. I was grateful for this secret place, to be sharing it with someone who didn't hurry me.

Like a tree house perched on stilts, the lifeguard station offered a panorama of the ocean, the pier, the amusement park, and the boardwalk.

"Do you know what I sometimes think?" I offered, studying the view from my perch on high.

Just above the rim of her glasses, Brenda's eyebrows lifted.

"I sometimes think that God has a view like this. When I'm up here, sometimes I think we are sharing this view together, just me and God."

Brenda was silent. Then she pulled a packet from her pocket and shook out a cigarette. She tilted the packet in my direction, spoiling the moment. "Want one?"

I shook my head.

Brenda struck a match and said, "I think mathematicians and physicists treasure views like this, too."

"Mathematicians and physicists?" I hoped my question hadn't sounded too harsh.

"When you get up high like this, you can clear your mind to see the patterns."

"Patterns?"

"Yes. Mathematics. It's the science of patterns." She took a deep drag from her cigarette. "Mathematics helps you see the patterns behind things. The outcome of the rolls of a dice. The voting trends of an election. The orbit of the planets."

I kept quiet. I didn't want to say that I saw no patterns whatsoever in mathematics. I saw only random letters and numbers flitting across the pages of my algebra book, looking like chicken scratchings.

Brenda tapped a long ash against the wooden side of the shelter. "Mathematics is something like an X-ray. It shows you the skeletons behind things."

I caught a flicker of understanding behind her words. "The way you put it," I said, "mathematics sounds a little like poetry. Expressing what you thought was inexpressible."

A look like dawn crossed Brenda's face. "That's right," she said. "I never thought of it that way." As a smile spread across her face, the tilted right side of her nose tipped up and away, like a tiny bird on the ascent.

Brenda and I talked about things I'd never spoken to anyone about before. After all, Sally and I had never spent any time really thinking together. But then something warm began spreading inside me, like butter when it begins to soften, then melt. The something was the sense that my almost-friend might become my all-the-way friend.

"What word would you use to describe this moment?" Brenda asked.

I was startled in the same way I had been when Brenda's father had asked whether I liked that odd painting in his shop. "What do you mean: '. . . *this moment*'?"

"You know, a moment when you start feeling a closeness with a person. Like you can trust. You know, be friends with them."

I was thrown off guard. I didn't know what to say. "It's hard to come up with just the right word for something. Especially so fast."

The sun had been dropping behind us, and the horizon ahead was streaked with a fragile shade of pink, which would soon turn to magenta. I stared at the ocean. "Maybe finding the right word is sort of like your anemometer. It takes awhile to gauge things precisely. In just the right way."

Brenda's grin filled her bright, round face. "Of course, Genevieve. I should have known you'd need some time to think about things."

Suddenly Brenda was off in a new direction; she was attempting to shinny up to the roof of the lifeguard stand.

Brenda made it to the top. She was now preparing to jump from the roof onto the sand.

"Be careful, Brenda!" I called.

Ignoring me, Brenda prepared to leap. She hung in the air for a moment as I held my breath. As soon as Brenda landed with her knees bent and her torso upright in a wet pillow of sand, I began to breathe again.

"Hey," she called from down below. "Since you can't think of your own word yet, I've got a new favorite word to share, Gen."

"You mean something to replace *pervert*?"

She nodded, brushing the sand from her legs.

"Yep," she shouted. "Something even better."

I could feel the bubbles of laughter rising inside me. Brenda was unpredictable. That was part of her charm.

"You got something to write with, Genevieve? It's kind of long."

I pulled out a pen from between the pages of my journal.

"Ready?" she called.

"Ready," I called back.

She called out the letters to me. It was the longest word I had ever heard. Before she darted across the sand and disappeared, I think I had written A-N-T-I-E-S-T-A-B-L-I-S-H-M-E-N-T-A-R-I-A-N.

Naturally, I would have to look it up in the dictionary.

17

The meeting set up for the Womperses to air their complaints had been rescheduled for the Thursday after the hurricane. Usually the monthly school board meetings were held in a small conference room beside the principal's office. Because a large crowd was expected at this one, however, the meeting had been moved to the cafeteria.

Hurricane Edna's legacy was one of rain. What I remembered most was sloshing with my parents through the ankle-high puddles in the school parking lot on our way to the meeting.

On the ride over in the car, I tried to tune out my father's mutterings. He had been going on about the Communists and the fair-weather patriots that seemed to characterize America nowadays. Now he was complaining that he'd have to give up his work in the backyard with Uncle Bud tonight. Our yard had been flooded by the storm, and Uncle Bud and my father had concocted homemade drainage systems to divert the water. They had made little progress over the last week.

Now, entering the cafeteria between my two parents, I noticed that the atmosphere was entirely different than it had been at noon. Although the lingering odors of sloppy joe sauce and bleach filled the cafeteria, the sounds of scraping chairs and laughing students were absent.

I looked over at my father sitting awkwardly in a student-sized chair, feeling a kind of relief as he changed subjects, muttering now about the Rosenbergs, the treasonous spies who had been executed just last year for providing nuclear secrets to the Russians.

Near the front of the cafeteria, where the ice-cream freezers were set up at noon, Mr. and Mrs. Wompers sat nervously.

Of late, Mr. Donner's shop had been closed for business as often as it had been open. The storm had caused little damage throughout the community, and Eastoners had returned quickly to work. But Mr. and Mrs. Wompers were concentrating on their presentation to the school board to the exclusion of everything else. I wondered how they ever intended to turn a profit.

In fact, Mr. and Mrs. Wompers had even consulted with me, claiming that I knew so much about the people in Easton. Brenda and I had watched as they had assembled their notes, arranged their presentation, and rolled the film clips they had brought from Hollywood. I told them what I thought: They should keep it simple, and they should rely on the film clips more than the lecture.

Brenda and I had been thrown together more and more often. There was the algebra tutoring, of course. But then there was the group project for social studies.

It had happened like this: In Mrs. Pagano's social studies class we had been studying the Salem Witch Trials. It was part of the unit on the colonial period in American history.

Spellbound, I absorbed Mrs. Pagano's information. In 1692, in Salem, Massachusetts, twenty-eight people had been convicted of being witches. Of that number, nineteen were hanged, and eighty-year-old Giles Corey was pressed to death. Even several dogs were accused of being witches.

As Mrs. Pagano had talked about Salem, it was hard to tell who the witches were. Were they the accused? The accusers? Did witches exist at all?

Mrs. Pagano began to assign topics like the colonial justice system, colonial superstitions, colonial religion, and others. Most of the girls chose partners quickly. Janice Neddeger and April Summers would be working together, and so would Iris Campbell and Renee Fedders. Brenda looked over at me. Glancing at the other girls, she mouthed the word *pervert*; I mouthed back *phony*.

Finally Brenda and I were the only ones without a topic or a partner. Mrs. Pagano smoothed over the situa-

tion. "Gen and Brenda," she said, "you two can work together on a topic of your choosing. With your combined
creativity, I'm sure you'll be able to come up with something original."

I wasn't so sure.

Often Brenda and I met up at the lifeguard station.
There I wrote and worked on algebra; there she fiddled
with her gauges and tutored me. Now we added our work
on the Salem Witch Trials to our time spent together.

We had quickly made the secret shelter our own.
Brenda began by carving her favorite word into the
wooden crossbars: *antiestablishmentarian.* I had looked
up this word in the dictionary. It described her perfectly:
"marked by opposition or hostility to conventional social,
political, or economic values or principles." I followed her
lead by carving *pervert* and *radioactive* and *nuclear* into
the walls of the shelter.

My algebra was improving. It helped when Brenda explained algebra in terms of things I could understand.

"It's easy to remember certain numbers, but not
others, right, Gen?"

I nodded. "Sure. I have no trouble remembering my
birth date, for instance. Or my phone number."

"Right. And that's because your birth date and your
phone number have *meaning* to you. Other numbers just
don't, so the trick is to get numbers to *mean* something
to you."

One time, Brenda opened a big sack of saltwater taffy to explain the principle behind this problem:

$$x + y = y + x$$

She took four pieces of saltwater taffy out of the bag. Then she lined them up at equal distances from each other along the ledge of the station.

I looked from left to right at a green, pink, yellow, and blue piece of taffy.

"Now," Brenda said, pointing to the candy, "aren't the green and pink pieces on the left equal to the yellow and blue pieces on the right?"

"Sure. That's easy."

"And if I switch them around? If I put them in a different order?"

I watched her move the pieces of candy. Now, from left to right, I eyed the pink, green, blue, and yellow pieces of taffy.

"The two on the left still equal the two on the right," I concluded. "They're just in a different order."

"Very good," she exclaimed, giving one of her anemometers a triumphant spin. "It's the exact same thing as the algebra problem. 'x plus y equals y plus x.' Only it's easier to understand when you think of the symbols as pictures or patterns to rearrange."

I continued to write my poetry at the lifeguard shelter, sometimes when Brenda was there, but more easily when she wasn't around. Mr. Henderson had been teaching us about rhymed verse and free verse, and he'd introduced us to poets as different as Tennyson and Emily Dickinson. We'd been given a long-term assignment. We were to keep a poetry notebook, and by the end of the poetry unit, we were to have produced ten original poems. I hadn't groaned about the assignment like the other students. In fact, I'd been trying my hand at various poetic styles: the tight imagistic style of Emily Dickinson; the religious conceits of John Donne; the swaggering, heroic style of Lord Byron; the undressed, capital-free style of e. e. cummings.

Our first poem was due the Monday after Edna passed over Easton. Mine had been inspired by the internal and external storms of the past several weeks.

As Mr. Henderson passed back the graded poems I squirmed nervously in my seat. Then I saw my grade: a large A scrawled in Mr. Henderson's broad, loopy handwriting. Hurriedly I scanned Mr. Henderson's comments in the margin, blushing at his praises: "I/eye image = Nice verbal acrobatics!"

At the end of class, Mr. Henderson motioned me to his desk.

"Given the weather we've experienced of late," he said, rising, "and your poetic interest in storms," he continued, "I thought you'd be interested in how Shakespeare described a storm."

He opened an old dog-eared paperback book. *King Lear* the title said. Then Mr. Henderson began to read:

Blow, winds, and crack your cheeks! rage! blow!
You cataracts and hurricanes, spout
Till you have drench'd our steeples, drown'd the cocks!

I didn't know what a cataract was, but I understood
how a hurricane raged and blew. And I liked the way
Mr. Henderson knew how to use his voice. The words
"drench'd" and *"drown'd"* rumbled out like thunder. I
wondered if I'd ever be able to read poetry out loud with
such passion.

"At any rate," he said, passing the thin volume to me as
the bell rang, "you can keep it for a while if you'd like. It's
my college copy of *King Lear,*" he said. "The storm's described in act three, scene two."

One windy afternoon at the lifeguard station, I shared
my A poem with Brenda. We had finished another challenging session of math, and she had helped me to see,
once again, that I would be able to pass Algebra I, even
though I'd probably never like it. I was grateful.

As I read, she listened intently.

Outside it is raging,
Buffeting me,
Flinging me from pole to pole.
It is ripping at my hair and
Shredding my eyes,
Ignoring the cries from my heart.

Facing its peril,
Bearing against its wind,
Ignoring its chilly damp,
I press on,
Seeking the still calm center
Of the I.

After I finished reading, Brenda got quiet, her curls entirely still. Then with a kind of reverence usually reserved for physics, she said, "Wow, Gen. I'll bet that took as long to write as it took me to build that new anemometer gauge."

She meant it as the sincerest compliment.

Then suddenly she was off, and I followed her, heading to the shoreline against the wind. We climbed onto the jetty, the stiff waves stinging our feet and ankles like salty nettles. From atop the sharp and slippery rocks, Brenda began to declaim the words from my poem, shouting my *-ing* words into the ocean. Soon, following Brenda's lead, I had joined in, swinging my arms in rhythm with hers as we cried my participles into the pounding surf: *buffeting, flinging, facing, seeking.* I had never uttered my own words aloud before.

Now, wiggling uncomfortably in my own plastic cafeteria seat, I noticed for the first time how hard it was. Glancing at my father, who was muttering to himself, I felt like a traitor. The fact was that having listened to the Womperses more carefully, I was beginning to change my mind about the Civil Defense program.

One afternoon after the storm, in the middle of a heated discussion about the Salem Witch Trials project, Brenda had suddenly blurted out, "My favorite part's the cities with the circles around them. What's yours?" That was Brenda Wompers: a quirky blend of seriousness and spontaneity.

I had wondered how Brenda Wompers could call the cities with the circles around them her favorite part. The Civil Defense officer made a practice of showing our classmates a huge map of the United States. Cities like Seattle and Omaha had big red bull's-eyes ringed around them, as if marked for target practice. The circles made me shudder.

"I like the house pictures, too," Brenda had said. "They're neat."

I had thought back to the house pictures the Civil Defense officer brought to school. One series of pictures showed a small house barely a mile from ground zero. When the bomb went off, the house was first scorched, then engulfed in flame, and finally shattered by a shock wave that ripped it to pieces.

"Only takes forty-seconds flat to rip that place to shreds!" Brenda had elbowed me in the ribs approvingly. "That's faster than it takes Janice Neddeger to spread a rumor!"

Lately, my days had been filled with Brenda's comical talk about the nuclear menace that preoccupied her parents. My nights, on the other hand, were filled with restless dreams; I had almost finished reading *Hiroshima,* and I could no longer fall asleep without the conch shell at my ear, the soothing sounds of the sea settling my thoughts about the Japanese citizens caught in the light of history's most ominous flashbulb.

Now the school board meeting was about to begin. Superintendent Teeters's secretary, Anita Mathers, moved to the record player to start "The Star-Spangled Banner." I saw Janice, April, Iris, and Renee slip away from their parents to gather together. Like the rest of the crowd, I rose as Mario Lanza began to sing, *"O say, can you see . . . ?"* I placed my hand over my heart as the needle scraped at the recording, and I felt hope rising in my heart the way it did whenever God and the flag were invoked with proper reverence and solemnity.

But then I glanced over at the tile walls. Someone had plastered signs all over the cafeteria. A few of them were familiar advertisements about the upcoming Halloween party. When I looked more closely, however, I saw that most of the signs were posters from Janice Neddeger's "Wonders of the Atomic Age" report. I felt my hope sink.

After "The Star-Spangled Banner" came the Pledge of Allegiance. Under the metal dog tag, I could feel my heart beating swiftly. I heard the words trail off: " . . . one nation, under God, indivisible, with liberty and justice for all." I wondered if "for all" was a synonym for "Neighbors All" and included Mr. and Mrs. Wompers, too.

Now it was time for the Womperses to begin their presentation. They began by thanking everybody, and then fumbled with the notes they had written so carefully. I glanced over at my mother, who was examining the Womperses with her predictably critical eye. I knew what she was thinking: She wanted to rush forward and pull up Mrs. Wompers's sagging hosiery and straighten Mr. Wompers's sloping bow tie.

I knew their facts were accurate. Reading secretly late at night, I pored over magazines like *Time* and *Collier's* that I had checked out of the school library and hidden from my parents in my book bag. Just like Mr. and Mrs. Wompers now did, the magazines stated the dreadful consequences of nuclear war: cars and trucks would be lifted and thrown like Molotov cocktails, spewing flaming gasoline, oil, and metal like shrapnel on a battlefield; in New York City, even a modest one hundred thousand bomb-related casualties would require six hundred thousand pints of blood over a six-week period; it would also take seventeen freight cars to carry that much blood to the injured.

Now Mr. and Mrs. Wompers turned to current events.

"I'm sure you are all aware of the incident of the *Lucky Dragon* of just last March," Mr. Wompers stated calmly.

I looked around at some of the others sitting near me

in the cafeteria. On their faces were either blank stares or outright confusion. Mr. Wompers had given us too much credit. He explained.

Just last March a Japanese fishing vessel, the *Lucky Dragon*, had been working about 85 miles from the United States government's hydrogen bomb test at Bikini Atoll. The test of the "Bravo" bomb ignited a blast that was 750 to 1,000 times more powerful than the atomic bomb dropped on Hiroshima. The blast gouged a crater in the reef that was almost a mile wide; within seconds the fireball was nearly 3 miles in diameter; the illumination from the blast was visible on an island 135 miles east of the explosion. Hours later, a curious white ash began falling on the *Lucky Dragon*. Several crew members collected bags of it as souvenirs. Before the end of the day, everyone on the ship was sick. The crew was hospitalized on its return to Japan. One of the crew members died.

Now Mr. Wompers turned the program over to his wife. "The *Lucky Dragon* incident," Mrs.Wompers explained, "alerted the world to the dangers of radioactive fallout."

I felt oddly ashamed. My newspaper-reading father had never mentioned the *Lucky Dragon*; neither had my copy of the *Weekly Reader*.

"No one yet realizes the dangers of fallout," insisted Mrs. Wompers. "It's important for us to protest atomic tests by our government," she urged, "to keep radioactive fallout from poisoning our citizens, our air, our water. People are building shelters to protect themselves from a bomb blast. They are teaching our young people to duck and cover. But even if anyone *should* survive a nuclear blast, which is nearly impossible, the fallout from the bomb's aftermath would surely kill or sicken them. People need to be *more* worried about *that* than about building bomb shelters to hide in."

Now the audience began to stir.

Robert Fedders rose to his feet. "What makes *you* such an expert on this subject, madam?" I noticed that he pronounced the word *madam* like a swift flick on a fanny with a locker room towel.

Mr. Wompers pushed back his narrow shoulders. "My wife worked for the Ryan Energy Institute, a think tank in Southern California. She was on the cyclotron team. It was her job to learn about these matters. She's a gifted scientist."

Now the audience grew restless, just as it did whenever Brenda talked in class about something we didn't know about.

"Yes," Mrs. Wompers continued. "I learned about a lot of things that aren't common knowledge. That sheep were dying mysteriously in Utah. That cattle herds suffered strange diseases. That 'blue snow' fell over areas surrounding the Nevada Proving Grounds. That children were complaining of swollen tongues."

Now Al Summers sprang to his feet. "Are you saying that the United States Atomic Energy Commission is *wrong*? Just last year it issued a report stating that the radioactivity released by fallout was not hazardous."

Now Mrs. Wompers ran her open palm across her forehead, sweeping her thick gray hair behind her ear. "Not only am I saying that the Atomic Energy Commission is *wrong*," she said, gathering her words carefully, "I'm saying that it is *lying*."

Now the room broke into an uproar. I wished that Mrs. Wompers had followed my advice. At their practice sessions I had suggested that she might want to let her husband do most of the talking tonight or to at least tone down her language. People in Easton didn't like women to overshadow their husbands or speak their minds strongly. But it wasn't that Mrs. Wompers hadn't listened. She had forgotten. I had seen it before; sometimes Mr. and Mrs. Wompers and their daughter Brenda entered a world all their own, a world with a population of three.

Brenda, sitting in the front row, jumped up. She saw that her parents were in danger of losing their audience's attention altogether. She attempted to salvage the situation.

"The film clips, *the film*," she said, motioning to Eddie Brinkley behind the projector. "Roll the *film*."

Eddie Brinkley turned on the projector, and it began to whir. Brenda streaked across the room, her black curls dancing, and flipped out the lights. While the film slowly unwound, Brenda explained to the audience that these clips were from a film called *Them!* Her father had received them in advance of release from friends in Hollywood. They were clips, she said, that underscored her parents' concerns.

I could feel the tension in the cafeteria pulling in two directions: away from a young woman who dared to address a crowd of adults and toward curiosity about a film honored by advance release in tiny Easton.

While the film rolled, I noticed that Brenda was not watching the movie; she was studying the faces of the other girls. Iris Campbell was knitting her brow as she learned that something terrible had happened in the desert of New Mexico. Renee Fedders's eyes widened as a traumatized young girl wandered away from a trailer that contained the bodies of her dead parents and had unusual footprints around it. Carol Calloway chewed on her fingernails as the suspense built and the little girl screamed, "THEM! THEM!"

When slowly it is revealed to the audience that the murderer is a gigantic creature, Janice and Renee clutched each other's hands. As the creatures looming over the desert dune are revealed to be giant mutated ants, Iris and April shrieked in unison.

I was almost as frightened as the other girls, even though I had seen these clips before, huddled in the dark room of the souvenir shop behind a black curtain.

On the screen, the giant ants, exposed to atomic radiation at the first atomic testing site in White Sands, New Mexico, have been transformed. They have mutated into 9- to 12-foot man-eaters. They invade the Los Angeles sewer system. As I watched the attacking mutants making frightening, cricketlike sounds I thought of Biblical prophecies about the destruction of the earth: . . . *and there shall be darkness come upon creation, and the Beasts shall reign over the earth.*

When the film clips ended, Brenda flipped the lights back on. "My dad says Hollywood's thinking about doing other 'bug' movies," Brenda announced, attempting to diffuse their fear with a light sprinkling of humor. "Flies. Leeches. Tarantulas."

The other students and a few of their parents shuddered and glanced at each other nervously.

Then Mr. and Mrs. Wompers stepped to the podium to continue the discussion, and Brenda sat down.

"What did you folks think of the film?" Mr. Wompers asked.

The room fell silent.

"No, really," Mrs. Wompers said encouragingly. "We really want to know what you think. At the end of the movie, FBI agent Graham asks, 'If the monsters got started as a result of the first atomic bomb in 1945, what about all the others that have been exploded since then?'"

"Yes," Mr. Wompers said, nodding along with his wife.

"What do you all think about that?" The corners of his mouth lifted hopefully.

Silence draped the room like blackout curtains.

Finally Janice Neddeger raised her hand. She stood up and answered quietly. "It's terrifying."

Now I heard Mrs. Wompers offer a familiar response to Janice. "My husband didn't ask you how you *felt* about it, dear," she said, not unkindly. "He asked you what you *thought* about it."

The other girls shifted in their plastic chairs. They bristled on Janice's behalf.

Like Mr. and Mrs. Wompers, I wanted to know what the other girls thought, too. I was tired of the way those girls acted in unison. I wanted to know what they really thought. Each one. Individually.

Suddenly Mr. Neddeger rose on his daughter's behalf. "Maybe Janice doesn't know *what* to think." I caught the angry way Carl Neddeger flung his hands and the sharp, cutting edge to his words. Carl Neddeger, Janice's father, owned the local furniture store, a place filled with the end tables and étagères my mother coveted. "In the movie Dr. Medford says that the bomb has opened the door into another world," Carl Neddeger continued. "Nobody can predict what will happen in that new world. What are we *supposed* to think about something like that?"

Mr. Wompers replied, "You're not *supposed* to think anything in particular. The fact that nobody can predict what will happen shouldn't prevent us from trying to think hard about solutions to the problem anyway."

I heard the grumbling around me. People were becoming hostile.

"We acknowledge," Mrs. Wompers quickly added, "that trying to think about these things produces a numbing effect. But the worst thing that can happen is if we allow ourselves to become apathetic, if we allow ourselves *not* to think about the consequences."

Members of the audience were beginning to strike up side conversations. One or two people even got up and left.

Over the restless and noisy crowd Mrs. Wompers tried to take another tack. "Don't you think there's any *truth* to the movie? Don't you think mutant creatures might be *possible* in the future?"

Now Larry Campbell, Iris's father, stood up. "That's ridiculous," he scoffed. "All those close-ups of antennae and hairy ant legs and bugged-out eyes. They're just in there to scare us. Just technical Hollywood effects."

"Yes," agreed Robert Fedders, shrugging. "It's just a scary movie. Pure entertainment. That's all."

Mrs. Wompers looked at Mr. Wompers. "Harry and I think it's more than just a scary movie," she said soberly. "We think it's possible that the radiation from nuclear bombs might result in a world just like this."

Now, fumbling with the papers which he'd gotten

hopelessly out of order, Mr. Wompers took up the consequences of radioactive fallout—on the environment as well as on people. "And if birds die off because of radiation sensitivity," Mr. Wompers continued, "the world would be left to radiation-resistant insects."

"Yes," said Mrs. Wompers. "It's possible that insects could plague the world."

"And the radiation," added her husband, "could get into the food supply. It could poison our cattle, our wheat fields. It could get into our babies' milk. Eventually it could even get into the milk of nursing mothers."

I noticed that Mr. and Mrs. Wompers had now entered that world above their heads, a world that seemed habitable by them alone.

Brenda stepped up before the audience again, reaching for the pamphlets her mother had passed out at the Welcome Wagon tea. She thrust them into the reluctant hands of the audience.

"Brenda's mother is proposing this petition campaign," said Mr. Wompers, gazing proudly at his wife. I noticed that his bow tie had slipped from a horizontal to a vertical position; whenever he spoke, the tip of the tie now brushed his chin like a bothersome fly.

"It simply asks that the Civil Defense curriculum incorporate a more realistic view of the consequences of nuclear testing and nuclear weaponry," Mrs. Wompers added.

Mrs. Wompers read the petition out loud. I focused on

the words that appealed most to me: *consequences, accuracy, correction.* "I'm hoping enough people will sign to allow for some changes."

"Well, *we* think," said Al Summers between snarled lips, "your ideas are hogwash!"

People applauded Al Summers and the applause encouraged him. "Every true American proudly supports our president. Every true American loyally supports our civil defense measures."

Now Carl Neddeger and Larry Campbell rose up, too. "Either you are committed to your nation's defense or you're not."

Al Summers went even further. "You know what they call *dis*loyal Americans, don't you?"

The crowd grew silent for a moment.

Then Carl Neddeger responded. "Communists is what they call 'em!"

"Yeah, *Communists!*" echoed Larry Campbell.

Then the air was punctuated with cries from all over the room. "Communists!" people shouted. "Communists!"

I heard my father muttering beside me. "That's right. If you're not committed, you become an open invitation to the Communists."

From where I sat, Mr. and Mrs. Wompers seemed, for the first time, very small, too small to have caused such an uproar. I don't know why I hadn't noticed this before; after all, I had often observed Mr. Wompers's narrow shoulders and Mrs. Wompers's round face enlarged only by her wild mane of hair. Not only did they now seem small, but they seemed somehow ridiculous. Mr. Wompers's bow tie had slipped from its moorings and spun back and forth at his neck like one of those whirligigs children held to the wind on the boardwalk, and Mrs. Wompers looked poorly dressed in her makeshift suit and sagging hose.

Suddenly Brenda was on her feet again; she was aware of how rapidly her parents had lost ground. "Don't you see?" she pleaded, shouting to make herself heard. "Nuclear catastrophe is like the hurricanes around here," she offered. The crowd quieted down a bit; they might not have understood nuclear catastrophe, but they understood hurricanes. "They're disasters. Their destruction can be devastating. You can't control them, yet that doesn't prevent you from taking precautions, for thinking about and preparing for what's likely to come."

I thought about my father and his weather maps. I thought about the hardware store and its storm season supply of plywood and batteries. I thought about Carl Neddeger and the furniture business that lagged during good weather but prospered during bad; when the furniture in Easton homes was ruined by hurricanes, people often purchased replacements in Carl Neddeger's store. Most of all, I thought Brenda Wompers must be a genius. Suddenly the audience had come to attention again.

"Thank you, dear," added Mrs. Wompers, regaining

her composure. "And *we* think that the school curriculum should at least acknowledge the negative consequences of nuclear energy. Talking about these things and preparing for them seems as reasonable to us as talking about and preparing for the hurricanes that may—or may not—strike."

Now Mr. Wompers spoke. "I thought it might be a good idea to enlist some young people to sign our petition, too," he added gamely. "It is, after all, their world that will be plunged into this terror."

The young people shifted uneasily in their hard chairs. They drummed their fingers on the table. They looked away from the podium.

"Here, Trish," said Mr. Wompers. "Here's a pen the young people and their parents might want to use."

Now, with a flourish, Brenda stepped up to the podium. She pushed her glasses back up on her nose. She shook her hand dramatically, calling attention to the pen she picked up. She held the pen aloft, squinting at it as if it were an expensive piece of jewelry under a jeweler's glass. Pluckily, Brenda smiled and said, "It's from Hollywood. Look. On the side it reads, 'Desilu Studios. Hollywood, California.'"

I caught a glimpse of Iris Campbell and Janice Neddeger. I watched their lips moving, mimicking Brenda. "Cal-i-*for*-nia," the lips said.

The crowd rose, ignoring Brenda. Their plastic chairs

scraped across the cold tile floor. They passed the flag standing at soldierly attention in the corner. They trampled on the spring green pamphlets that covered the floor like clumps of mulched grass. They grumbled, muttering phrases like "Communists" and "fellow travelers." No one in the audience moved in the direction of the Hollywood pen.

The petition lay limply on the table. Mr. and Mrs. Wompers's stricken faces watched the members of the Easton community, neighbors all, marching steadily out of the building.

I now had someone to eat lunch with, but when Brenda and I sat together in the lunchroom, we were a target for harassment.

On the day after the school board meeting, the swarm of girls led by Janice Neddeger passed by our lunch table shrieking, "THEM! THEM!" Afterward, they moved to the far end of the cafeteria, doubled over with laughter and pointing in our direction.

The pointing made me shudder. It reminded me of the reading I'd been doing about the Salem Witch Trials. The young girls in Salem like Elizabeth Parris and Abigail Williams had been about the same age as my classmates. They had pointed their fingers at Sarah Good, Sarah Osborne, and the Carib Indian slave Tituba. Their fingers had labeled these women as witches and eventually led to nineteen deaths.

Soon after, April Summers led the group in a stroll past our table. Suddenly she tripped, and her tray of spaghetti spilled all over us, the spiraling strands of spaghetti trailing down our blouses. Then April pointed to the splotches of red tomato stains on our blouses. "Reds! Pinkos!" April shouted. Soon the students up and down the table picked up the chorus, "Reds! Pinkos!" They held their sides with laughter.

I hated the names they called Brenda and me: *Red, pinko, Commie sympathizer, fellow traveler.* I didn't even know what all the names meant, but I understood their intent well enough.

I had looked up *Communist* in the dictionary. "Noun," it explained. "One who is a member of the Communist party." There it was, clear as day. If you were a Communist, you—or others—could prove it with a card. All it took to establish your status as a card-carrying Communist was a membership card. And if you denied it, your accuser could go look for your name on a membership list somewhere.

I had asked Brenda directly. "Are you a Communist, Brenda?"

"No."

"What about your father?"

"No."

"Your mother?"

"No."

"Have any of you ever *been* Communists in the past?"

"No."

I believed her.

"But doesn't it bother you that they call you that name?" It bothered me terribly. Every noon while Brenda and I ate, Janice and her friends fixed us with their eyes, staring at us as if we were specimens of beetles laid out in an entomologist's specimen box. *Communist pinko* was the genus and species we'd been given.

"You can be certain, Genevieve," she said earnestly, attempting to reassure me, "that the only party I claim allegiance to is the party of the antiestablishmentarians."

The worst indignity occurred one lunchtime when Brad Connors appeared beside Brenda and me, hovering over us like a shaggy, lumbering bear. He held up a glass jar. Then he unscrewed the lid, and a jarful of roaches ran madly in all directions across the tabletop in front of us. From nearby, student voices chorused, "Them! Them!"

Brenda laughed off these dirty tricks. But I couldn't.

"Don't pay any attention to them, Gen," Brenda insisted. "Besides, I think my physics project may help us out."

"Your *physics* project?" Sometimes I didn't understand Brenda Wompers at all.

"It's coming along nicely. I've got the three Easton UFO sightings set up as experiments in my room. The one that's likely the weather balloon. The one that's likely the planet Venus. And the third one, the Janice Neddeger sighting. The one with the spaceship and the portholes on that night of her wreck. I'm still having a bit of trouble explaining that third one."

She looked across the cafeteria at the other students, who were pointing and giggling at us. I knew that look. Brenda may have been looking, but she wasn't seeing. Instead, she was likely concentrating on her physics project, staring off, as if her eyes possessed a kind of X-ray vision to penetrate the mysterious patterns in the world.

Suddenly Brenda turned to me and blurted out: "Genevieve, how good is Iris Campbell with a camera?"

I thought back to the campaign for class secretary last spring. "Iris is good with a camera, Brenda. It's been her hobby for years. She used her skills against Sally last year."

I explained how Iris had snapped unbecoming photos of Sally to use in the campaign against Janice Neddeger. Sally with her mouth open at the class picnic. Sally with her arm around Wills on the boardwalk. Sally buried under the sand at the beach, squinting against the sun. Iris had created an unflattering montage of photographs. But I told Sally the trick would backfire. I knew nearly everyone in our class had a picture of themselves they wouldn't like paraded before the world, and I predicted they'd sympathize with Sally. I was wrong.

I turned to Brenda. "Why would Iris do such mean things to Sally?"

Brenda looked irritated. "Remember the scorpion and the frog?"

I nodded.

"It's in her nature, Genevieve."

Sometimes I avoided Brenda at lunchtime. One noon I hid out in the library instead of eating lunch. On another day I sat on the toilet in the restroom, munching my sandwich behind the locked stall door. Like the hermit crab, I sought shelter after shelter in which to hide, but I was ashamed of my behavior.

Still, Brenda never criticized me for my cowardice. She seemed content to let me go my way, for she certainly intended to go hers.

19

I knew my mother's Tupperware party was under way when she challenged one of the guests to a game of catch.

This time Nancy Summers volunteered.

I watched my mother fill the Tupperware Wonder Bowl to the top with water and then seal it tightly.

"Now, Nancy," she gloated, holding the heavy bowl high, "I guarantee that I can throw this bowl across the room to you without any spilling, dripping, cracking, leaking, or breaking open."

Nancy Summers looked skeptical. She didn't want to damage anything in Yvonne Campbell's living room. Mrs. Campbell's living room was filled with the newest modern furniture. There was a boomerang-shaped coffee table, a Danish modern telephone table, and a chaise lounge that looked like a psychiatrist's couch. The sleek shapes of metal and plastic were the latest in home fashions, but they seemed cold to me.

Still, recalling the contrast between Brenda's disordered room at her home and Mrs. Campbell's perfectly appointed living room, I grinned silently.

Brenda had become obsessive about her physics project.

Just yesterday, I had been sitting in her room in what she called the Venus station. Brenda had explained that most of the UFO sightings were ordinary astronomical objects. They were simply planets or stars that glowed especially brightly. The Venus station had graphs and charts documenting this fact. She had graphs coordinating the maximum brilliance of Venus with reported saucer sightings. She had newspaper articles about World War II pilots who had wasted rounds of ammunition firing at Venus, believing it to be enemy aircraft.

"I'm going to reject any explanation that has to do with autokinesis," Brenda had announced. "Don't you think?"

"What's that?"

I hadn't been able to follow her exactly. But it had something to do with the brain. The brain, Brenda had said, sometimes invested stationary lights with motion.

"And I'm doubtful that Saint Elmo's fire provides a theory worth pursuing."

I'd never heard of Saint Elmo's fire. It sounded like a name for a fire-eater's act up at the carnival beside the boardwalk. Brenda had explained that it had something to do with electricity. Something about positive charges giving off a reddish glow.

In the final analysis, I suppose I believed what most of

the people in Easton did: UFOs were Russian spy planes attempting to gather information about America's nuclear preparedness.

Now Mrs. Campbell nodded her approval to my mother's Tupperware challenge. Mrs. Summers stretched out her hands and held her breath. After my mother hurled the Wonder Bowl successfully into Mrs. Summers's outstretched hands, the other guests burst into wild applause.

The next part of the party routine was to challenge another volunteer to stand on a Tupperware canister to demonstrate the strength of Tupperware plastic. I watched as Diane Calloway placed one high-heeled foot atop a pastel pink canister, steadying herself by holding on to my mother's white-gloved hand. Then Mrs. Calloway lifted her other leg, setting the second heel firmly atop the Tupperware pinnacle.

As the gathered guests applauded again, my mother swept her hands across the myriad canisters, bowls, tumblers, containers, and utensils gathered on Yvonne Campbell's dining room tabletop like sacred objects on an altar. "Now you know, ladies," she said, smiling, "why Tupperware is 'Better by Far than Can or Jar.'"

Often I helped my mother with her Tupperware parties. Her sample case weighed nearly fifty pounds, and at a successful party she struggled to fill orders, keep the records, and make change.

This party took place about ten days after the school board meeting. As the women gathered around my mother's display, picking up catalogs and consulting order forms, I overheard many conversations spurred by the provocations of the Wompers family.

"We've got to believe our government," insisted Virginia Fedders, fingering a Tupperware ice cube tray. "Renee's Civil Defense pamphlet says a nuclear bomb's just another kind of explosion."

"You're right," agreed Anita Perkins. "It's just like a great big blast of TNT."

"And in the event of a disaster, we're protected by all the new interstate highways that can help us speed safely out of town," offered Blanche Millikin.

"Or if we want to stay close to home, we can escape to the shopping center that will double as an evacuation center."

"Besides," said Mrs. Campbell, stepping up to restore order to the display that now looked like the disarrayed card tables after a church rummage sale, "all kinds of good things have come from the atom."

"Yes, Yvonne," purred Eloise Neddeger, "the atom's energy is just perfect for generating power."

"And getting us to the moon," agreed Anita Perkins excitedly.

The latest *Weekly Reader* article had featured the nation's excitement about going to the moon. A sidebar had discussed Walt Disney's new theme park, set to open next year. One of the areas, called Tomorrowland, would feature rocket ships and astronauts blasting into outer space.

"And that horrible couple from California failed to mention our government's Atoms for Peace program," offered Eloise Neddeger with a shudder. "People like that just won't admit to the sunny side of the atom."

Mother and her friends could wring sunshine from disaster.

I looked at the plastic items in my mother's display. Perhaps Tupperware could seal out the fallout of radiation. Perhaps its futuristic powers of containment could prevent the threat of contamination. Perhaps Tupperware, I mused sunnily, looking over the cereal bowls and water tumblers, could serve as a bulwark against both contamination *and* Communism.

Now, however, I overheard gossip that involved me.

"Had you heard, Martha, that they're whispering about your daughter?"

"*Genevieve?*"

"They're saying she's a 'fellow traveler.'"

I winced at the indefinite "they." It seemed that anonymous "theys" caused a great deal of trouble in the world.

"What?" I heard the hollow sound of my mother's wedding ring banging against the polished table. "Genevieve's no Communist."

"I don't know," Eloise Neddeger hinted broadly. "She certainly travels in those circles."

"*What* circles?" gasped my mother.

"That Brenda Wompers. That Communist girl. Janice says Gen hangs out with her in school," announced Mrs. Neddeger.

"That's ridiculous. She's just tutoring Gen in math. There's nothing Communistic about Algebra I."

Now attempting to regain her composure, my mother rapped on the side of a Tupperware cereal bowl with a Tupperware pickle fork, calling the guests back to their seats.

I was familiar with this part of the party, too.

"It's the time in the program, girls," she went on, "when I get to teach you ladies about the 'bowls that burp.'"

I watched as my mother handed each guest a Wonder Bowl, then demonstrated the process. "First, you push down on the center of the seal to engage the lip with the edge of the bowl," she said, surveying the room.

"Then, you press down and just 'wink' the edge of the seal." Now my mother winked at her audience in anticipation of the event to come. After she winked the edge of her seal, it emitted the famous Tupperware burp. "Hear that, ladies?" she crowed with satisfaction.

Now while the ladies all burped their bowls in unison,

giggling with delight, my mother went on about the virtues of Tupperware.

"It won't scratch your shelves or countertops," she glowed. "Its edges won't cut or bruise your children," she enthused. "It won't break or crack like glass. It won't leave rust marks. Tupperware's the 'polite' kind of plastic."

Now Blanche Millikin spoke up. "Except for that *burp*," she quipped, sending the room into gales of laughter and applause.

Next my mother solicited testimonials from other satisfied Tupperware customers. Nancy Summers liked the neatness of her ketchup dispenser. Eloise Neddeger liked the way her Cake Taker kept the bugs and ants away at a picnic. Anita Perkins liked using the Ice-Tups to make Popsicle treats for her children, although I had heard my mother on the phone saying you could freeze a few daiquiris for yourself in them, too.

In between testimonials the conversation turned to the Wompers family.

"They've just *got* to be Communists, don't you think, Nancy?"

"Absolutely. They never attempt to socialize, do they? They just kind of stick together."

"You're right. They don't seem to be joiners, Anita. I've never seen a single one of them at the YMCA, and not a soul has seen them show up at any church in town."

"Well, there's one thing they've surely joined, Yvonne. And that's the Communist party."

"I think they're trying to scare us with all that voodoo science."

"That's right, Eloise. Anything you'd ever want to know about the end of the world is right there in the Bible."

"It would be awful to think of an Easton that had gone over to those Communists, wouldn't it, Blanche?"

"What would life be like here if there were no God-fearing Americans around?"

I felt a universal shudder pass through the room.

Finally it was time for a game. Sometimes my mother brought items on a tray for the ladies to remember in the Memory Game. Sometimes my mother suggested the Hubby Game. In this game the ladies wrote imaginary newspaper advertisements describing their husbands' traits as if offering their spouses for sale. At one Tupperware party my mother had written her own advertisement about my father: "For Sale. One sobersided husband. Will swap for a single evening of rollicking laughter."

Tonight she suggested the Gossip Game.

The idea of the Gossip Game was to whisper a phrase in one person's ear. Then that person whispered the phrase into the next person's ear and then so on around the room. The idea was to see how the original phrase was altered as it moved from mouth to ear, from person to person around the room.

I was familiar with the phrase Mother used for the Gossip Game: "A stitch in time saves nine." She began by whispering it into the ear of Yvonne Campell, the night's hostess.

In the final version of the Gossip Game, those words were no longer "a stitch in time saves nine" but "a witch, in time, serves the Communist line."

20

I worried about Brenda's parents.

Curiosity seekers began appearing at the door of the souvenir shop, suspiciously appraising not only the odd merchandise but the owners as well.

"That painting looks like it's from that weird artist," said Blanche DeMarco. "You know, the one that just stands over the canvas and squeezes paint onto it straight from the tube?"

Nina Todvine, her friend, answered. "Yes. I think that was Jackson Pollock, dear. Wasn't he a Communist?"

Blanche DeMarco nodded. "All those artists are."

When Ralph Girard dropped by, he asked Mrs. Wompers, "Where are the coconut patties?"

Mrs. Wompers shrugged. "We've got them in a bin in the back," she said, pointing out the bin along the back wall. "We want to get rid of sweets in here eventually," she offered.

"Why?" taunted Ralph Girard. "Don't Communists believe in chocolate?"

But I was grateful to see Aunt Minna's smiling, round face looking over the thrift shop goods as Silver squawked, "Top o' the morning. Good *day*." I proudly introduced her to Brenda and to Mr. and Mrs. Wompers.

"Finally, there's a place in Easton where a body doesn't have to spend an arm and a leg for something to wear," she declared, hugging me and warming the shop with her smile. I loved Aunt Minna's fresh-scrubbed pink smell of Camay soap.

Aunt Minna held up a black leather belt and asked, "Do you think I could ask Bud to wear something other than his battered brown belt, Genevieve?"

"I don't know, Aunt Minna," I replied. "You know how he loves that old thing. Matter of fact, I don't think I've seen him wear another one in all the years I've known him!"

"Exactly right, dear," Minna said, stepping to the counter to pay for her purchase. "I'd like him to freshen up for that confirmation of yours and Wills'. It's just around the corner."

She was right. Our confirmation ceremony was coming up in early November. Wills and I and the other confirmands were attending once-a-week sessions instead of the every-other-week ones now. The other girls had been buzzing about what to wear. Janice and Renee and Iris had been taken by their mothers to Raleigh to shop for their white dresses. Renee had bought a white lace dress, and

Iris had bought one in white organdy. Both described the oodles of crinolines that billowed their skirts and made them feel as if they were floating on clouds.

When Wilma Turner and I tried to step closer to overhear their conversation more clearly, the other girls moved away. I'd seen Wilma's mother shopping in the used clothing section of the Womperses' shop for a dress for her daughter. My mother was making mine. My evenings were filled with endless fittings, measurings, and tuckings of a dress I hated; my mother had chosen white dotted swiss, a fabric with the blandness of tapioca pudding.

"I didn't know you were a churchgoer, Genevieve," Mr. Wompers said, genuinely surprised.

"Well," I stuttered, wanting to withdraw like the hermit crab into the security of silence, "it's not something you blab about much to others. It's kind of private, don't you think?"

Now Mrs. Wompers stepped forward. "Actually, Genevieve, we don't think very much about it."

Aunt Minna's eyes were wide.

"We're not what you'd call religious," confirmed Mr. Wompers. "But Trish and I have often wondered if we should have exposed Brenda to a number of religions at some time or another. As part of a full and complete education, you know."

Now Brenda stepped into the conversation, the straight black line of her glasses underscoring her seriousness.

"Yes, maybe I've been deprived in some way, don't you think, Gen?"

I nodded, and so did Aunt Minna.

"Still," Brenda went on, "the time to do that kind of exploring would have been more appropriate in California. In California we had a lot more religions than they do here in Easton. Buddhists. Jehovah's Witnesses. Muslims."

Aunt Minna fiddled with the belt buckle for Uncle Bud that she was holding in her hand. "Well, Brenda," she added helpfully, "we have a lot of religions here in Easton, too. We've got Presbyterian, Catholic, Southern Baptist, United Methodist."

Now Brenda piped up. "But aren't those just separate *churches*?" she asked. "You know, separate *denominations*? Those aren't really separate *religions,* are they?"

"Oh, well," conceded Aunt Minna a bit unsteadily, "I suppose that's true."

"Can I ring up that belt for you today?" Mr. Wompers asked, returning to business.

"That would be lovely." Aunt Minna smiled at Mr. Wompers. I was grateful for that smile. I hadn't seen anyone else in Easton smile at Mr. or Mrs. Wompers since the school board meeting. "I've always admired folks with a head for business," she added kindly, stroking the cat, which had curled up next to the register.

I was struck by the irony of her statement. Someone with a head for business wouldn't have banished the romance and western paperbacks from the shelves. Someone with a head for business wouldn't have opened and closed the shop at will.

"Yes, I suppose it's not for the faint of heart," Mr. Wompers said, brightening.

Mrs. Wompers began chattering again with Aunt Minna while her husband rang up the purchase. "Why," she rambled on, "would we insist on exposing our daughter to religion if we don't believe in religion ourselves?"

Brenda was nodding, agreeing with her mother's logic.

I stared at Mr. and Mrs. Wompers in disbelief. Did they have no sense of propriety? They could read books aplenty. But could they read *people*?

I looked at the flush on Aunt Minna's round cheeks and the awkward way she fumbled with her bag. Did they have no conception of how other people lived and thought?

"Good luck with your shop, sir," Aunt Minna said, addressing Mr. Wompers.

Mr. Wompers smiled back. "We appreciate your business. Come again."

As she left, the doorbell tinkled behind her, and Silver squawked, "Top o' the mornin'. Good *day!*"

21

Mr. and Mrs. Wompers became front-page news in the *Easton Eagle* the next week. Breakfast at our house was an ordeal the day the article appeared as my father rattled the pages and fired off the bullets of his commentary. I secretly saved the discarded newspapers to pore over later on in my room. Lou Marchesco, the reporter-photographer, had done some sleuthing out in California, and in the pages of the paper I discovered that a cyclotron had something to do with acceleration and particle generation and that Mr. Wompers had managed script production for a brief time at Desilu Studios.

But I was uncomfortable with the way the *Easton Eagle* was slanting the story. I especially disliked the unflattering photographs of Mr. and Mrs. Wompers blown up across its pages. Mr. and Mrs. Wompers were clearly uncomfortable before the cameras, and the portraits made them look suspicious, even cagy. There was one of a bespectacled Mr. Wompers standing over the thrift store merchandise as if they were stolen goods, the light glinting off his glasses and blurring the eyes behind them. There was another of Mrs. Wompers studying her green brochure, her tangled corona of hair suggesting a witch consulting a book of potions. I worried about the success of the souvenir shop. It was all reminding me of the Salem project for school.

At night, alone in bed, I also read more and more about the victims at Salem. Their simple, almost childlike names had become familiar to me: Sarah Good, Rebecca Nurse, Susannah Martin, Martha Corey. I had read their pleas before the magistrates, and in their words I heard the futility of challenging the allegations. Mary Bradbury asserted, "I do plead not guilty. I am wholly innocent of such wickedness." Bridget Bishop proclaimed, "I am no witch. I am innocent. I know nothing of it." Martha Carrier cried out, "I am wronged. It is a shameful thing that you should mind these folks that are out of their wits."

I turned to my Bible, too, staying up late, praying and meditating over the questions that troubled me: Why did people insist on bearing false witness? What was the point of their rumors and gossip?

Still, by day it was a challenge to have Brenda Wompers as an all-the-way friend.

Brenda had taken to wearing a red beret of late. She'd

preferred it to the black one. "More provocative," she announced. "More *antiestablishmentarian*," she said ironically. I could see her smirk through the cloud of cigarette smoke as we walked along the beach with Gunner and Wills.

Since the conversation with Aunt Minna at the souvenir shop, she'd been asking a lot of questions about religion. I was happy to answer. As her parents hadn't been churchgoers, I figured Brenda's education lacked a great deal if it hadn't included religious experiences. I tried to explain to her about the things I believed in: the authority of the Bible, the life of the hereafter. She had a lot of trouble understanding about the Trinity.

"You means it's *three* people, right, Gen?"

I nodded my head. "But it's not exactly *people*, Brenda. The Trinity refers to God the Father, Jesus his Son, and the Holy Spirit."

Then Brenda tilted her head and asked, "So are the three things considered as one? Or is the one considered as three things?"

"It's not one or the other. It's kind of both at the same time."

Brenda snapped her fingers, getting it. "It's like one of those trick pictures the psychologists use. In the same picture you can see either the outline of a wineglass or the face of a woman, right?"

I didn't like the way she compared the Trinity to a "trick picture," but I supposed she was on the right track.

In fact, I didn't always like the way Brenda questioned me about my faith.

One day, the sea was rough, and it was matched by squalls. I felt the wind blowing stiffly at my back, the strands of my hair snapping at my cheeks. We had taken Gunner along with us, and Brenda struggled to throw a stick to him into the face of the wind.

"I've been thinking that your religion has a lot to do with our Salem Witch Trials project." She tossed the statement out absently.

"*Your religion.*" The way she said it reminded me of other things I'd heard from the Womperses: *Your principal. That school of yours.* I felt pulled up short, like a puppy snapped on a choke chain. "How in the world can my religion have anything to do with the Salem Witch Trials, Brenda?"

"Well, you know, if witches aren't real, then God can't be real, either."

What was she talking about? "It's not an algebra problem, Brenda," I argued, "with God on one side of the equation and Satan on the other." I explained that I'd been reading a poet called e. e. cummings and a book of his poems whose title I loved. The poetry collection was called *is 5*. In it, cummings exults in the claim that poets have an advantage over everyone else. A poet is not limited to conventional knowledge, to facts like two plus two equals four. A poet can imagine *beyond* two plus two is four. A poet can fly across that boundary into a world in which two plus two can equal five.

But Brenda seemed to be only half listening. She was struggling to gauge the gusting wind, to throw the stick at an angle that would reach Gunner prancing downwind of us.

"What about your own Rule for Thinking, Brenda Wompers?" I shouted into the wind. "Have you forgotten the one that says an idea is not necessarily false because you would hate to believe it?"

But she didn't hear me. Instead, she was streaking after the stick, tossing up high wakes of sand, hoping to catch it ahead of Gunner.

I was irritated at Brenda Wompers. Maybe I was irritated at her parents, too. After all, I'd listened patiently to her ideas about nuclear war. Shouldn't she listen patiently to my ideas about God?

22

renda insisted that I meet her outside the Sweet Shop. "Four o'clock sharp," she whispered conspiratorially. It had something to do with the final touches on her flying saucer project.

"Brad Connors is working now," she said as I met her underneath the Sweet Shop sign. I had always liked that sign. The two S's of SWEET and SHOP were linked one on top of the other like the shape of a double-dipped ice-cream cone.

"I'm going to distract Brad," Brenda went on, "so I can put you to work."

"*Me*?"

"Yes," she insisted. "This is all in the interest of science," she said. The straight line of her glasses underscored the seriousness of her intent. "You're not going to let down the cause of science, are you?"

I gulped. I admitted my respect for science had grown since I'd met Brenda. In fact, I had begun listening to my father's newspaper reading a bit more carefully. I was even paying attention to the scientific content.

"Listen to this, Martha," he had said just this morning. He had shaken the pages of the newspaper to straighten them out, then folded them carefully into quarters so he could isolate the article he had been most interested in reading.

"Hmmmm?" my mother had said, not listening. She was spooning coffee from the Tupperware decanter into the paper filter of the coffeepot.

"It seems they're about to come out with a new report. They think they've found a direct connection between smoking cigarettes and lung cancer," he had announced. "Some researchers have just finished studies." Then he had turned to me, his somber mouth turned down into a deep scowl like the tragedy mask that advertised the school plays. "That's another reason why you'd dare not take up smoking, Genevieve."

I had nodded, feeling guilty in spite of my innocence. I wondered if Brenda's smoking was another guilt-by-association evil I could be tied to.

After breakfast, when I had clipped the article about smoking to share with Brenda later, I realized that something about me had changed. For the first time I was thinking about the connections between scientific research and real life. That was not something I had ever done before meeting Brenda and her parents.

Still, my respect for science was a tiny mouse next to Brenda's elephantlike obsession with it.

"Your job is to observe the revolving pie case," Brenda stated matter-of-factly.

"The revolving *pie case*?"

I was familiar with the revolving pie case. It was a large, five-tiered glass-enclosed case that displayed the Sweet Shop's pies for the day: coconut cream pies, Dutch apple pies, chocolate cream pies, sour cherry pies, lemon meringue pies. "What does the revolving pie case have to do with anything, Brenda?"

"It has to do with my physics project and the cause of science," she said, holding her head aloft in a kind of regal conceit.

"What do you want me to do?"

"I want you to figure out how fast the case is turning."

"How do I do that?"

Brenda's eyes held disappointment. "Haven't you learned *anything* from my anemometer experiments?"

"Of course I have." Brenda's anemometers were crowding the lifeguard shelter. She'd set up large anemometers and small anemometers, complicated gauges and simple gauges. I had learned that science required a lot of equipment.

"So, then," she said, challenging me, "how might you measure the speed of the revolutions, Gen?"

"Well, I guess I could count," I offered. "I know you

can figure out how far away a storm is by counting by one thousands."

Brenda's curls began to bounce. "I'd never heard of that before." She was genuinely curious.

"Well, *after* the lightning flash but *before* the thunderclap, you count. One thousand and one, one thousand and two, one thousand and three. Etcetera." I figured she hadn't heard of this system because she had lived in California where they didn't have storms. "If you get to three, the storm is three miles away; if you get to two, the storm is two miles away—"

Brenda interrupted, "and if you get to one, you'd better have taken shelter." Her face was awash in a grin. "That's a good start, Gen. But what are the two points you're going to count against? With the revolving dessert case?"

"Two points?"

"Yes. You began counting about the storm between two points. Between the lightning strike and the thunderclap. What two points will you use to measure the speed of the dessert case?"

"Oh." I wasn't sure.

"Well, you'll figure it out. I have faith in you. Now let's go in."

The bell rang as we opened the door. The sound chimed in my heart: *"You'll figure it out. I have faith in you."*

Brenda easily distracted Brad Connors. The Sweet

Shop gave out free samples on tiny wooden spoons, and Brenda was taking full advantage.

I went over to the display case. I saw the whipped cream on the coconut cream pie floating by on paper doilies. I saw the cinnamon sprinkles on the crust of the apple pie passing like freckles on a young boy's face. I watched the display case revolve, and my mouth watered.

Then I tried to figure out something to measure against.

The handle on the outside of the case, a round aluminum knob, seemed a good marker. And perhaps the broken pastry crust at the edge of the cherry pie might make another marker as well.

But I decided to practice first. I lined up my nose at the knob and waited for the broken pastry crust to line up with the knob, too. Then I'd count how long it took the broken crust to get back to the knob again after one full rotation. One thousand and one, I counted. One thousand and two.

"Can I help you, Genevieve?"

Drat. Brad Connors had ruined my counting. "No, thanks," I said, trying to hide my irritation. "Just looking."

"Well, if you're that hungry, Genevieve," he said, "I can give you a taste. Your nose is practically glued to the glass."

"No, thank you." Now I stepped back a little to keep

from pressing my nose to the case. It was going to be harder to count with my eyes farther back from the knob.

Brenda interrupted. She was tapping loudly on the counter. "You have a customer here," she insisted.

Brad sighed and lumbered over to her. That great big boy looked ridiculous in that teeny-tiny paper hat.

"I'd like to sample the fudge ribbon now, please."

I suppressed a giggle. In the background I'd already heard Brenda asking for samples of the lemon chiffon, the coffee brandy, and the butterscotch brickle.

I started my counting again. I lined up the knob and the broken pastry edge. One thousand and one. One thousand and two. One thousand and three. I got all the way to twelve before the broken pie crust edge made a full circle back to the aluminum knob.

I ambled over to Brenda. "Twelve," I whispered in her ear.

"Good work, Gen," she said.

Then, as she turned to go, Brad Connors asked, "Would you like anything, Genevieve?"

I shook my head. "No," I said. "Thanks, though."

"They've got samples," Brenda reminded me.

Brad Connors scowled. First he'd spent time giving out samples to Brenda. If she had her way, now he'd be giving out samples to me. And we weren't likely to buy a single scoop.

"Sure," I said, glancing over at the cherry pie with the broken crust in the revolving case. "How about a sample of cherry vanilla?"

Brenda and I tried to keep from laughing as we left the Sweet Shop. As soon as we got outside, we exploded into giggles.

23

That evening at Brenda's house, I began to understand her plan.

"Experiment three," she announced dramatically, "investigates that photograph of the UFO by Iris Campbell from April nineteen fifty-four."

Mr. and Mrs. Wompers had helped her set up the experiment. I couldn't make much sense of it. Along a tabletop had been set a banana-split dish, a mound of clay, a toothpick, and a battered camera. Behind the table was a backdrop of black poster paper.

"I'm figuring out just exactly how Iris and Janice faked that photograph."

"Faked?" My instincts had told me that the photograph might be faked. I just didn't see how. "But photographs don't lie."

"Seeing is not necessarily believing, Gen," Brenda cautioned.

Mrs. Wompers spoke up, defending her daughter.

"People misuse science all the time. They fake experiments. Or doctor them. It's shameful."

Mr. Wompers now beamed at Brenda proudly. "Our daughter, Genevieve, has taken on one of science's biggest challenges. Brenda is attempting to disprove something everybody else believes with certainty."

"Yes. That's what Galileo did," said Mrs. Wompers.

"And Isaac Newton."

"And Einstein."

I looked over at Brenda's tilted nose, curlicued hair, and distracted expression, imagining that visage on a painting in a museum collection portraying science's immortals. The image didn't quite fit. Yet.

Mr. Wompers repeated his theme. "It is easier to prove something than to disprove something everyone else believes."

I nodded. At Salem, it had been impossible to disprove you were a witch. At the lunch table, it had been impossible to disprove that you were a Communist. On the playground, it had been impossible to disprove that you were a retard.

"As you will see, Genevieve," said Brenda, stepping between her parents to get on with things, "there's nothing easier to fake than a UFO hoax."

I watched as they put the elements of the experiment together. It seemed, in a sense, like a family play performed for my benefit. I envied the togetherness it demonstrated.

First, Mr. Wompers rounded off the top of the banana-split dish with the mound of modeling clay; it took on a saucerlike shape.

Then, Mrs. Wompers stuck the toothpick in the top of the clay mound; it looked like an antenna.

Then, Mr. Wompers stuck black gumdrops into the sides of the clay; they looked like portholes.

Brenda held up the newspaper photograph from last April. Against the black poster board their saucerlike creation certainly looked like the shape depicted in the newspaper photo.

Then Brenda held up a set of more recent photographs. They depicted the experimental banana-split dish crowned with modeling clay, garnished with a toothpick, and decorated with gumdrops. "These are the pictures Mom and Dad and I have already taken. They're remarkably similar to Iris Campbell's photograph."

I looked closely. Brenda was right; they were pretty close to the newspaper photos.

"Only there's one problem," Brenda announced. "The newspaper photo makes the dish look like it's spinning. It gives you a sense of motion."

My eyes traveled back and forth between the newspaper photos from last April and Brenda's more recent pictures. She was right again.

"That's where you come in, Gen," Brenda declared.

"*Me*?"

"Sure. You and the rotating glass display case. You see, those three—Brad, Iris, and Janice—faked those photographs. Brad Connors was there that night. Wills said so. Only Brad ran away. So out of guilt, I think he helped those girls fake those pictures."

My mind was racing like it often did around Brenda, huffing to keep up.

"And he had the key to the Sweet Shop. And access to the banana-split boats and the rotating pie case. And I'm assuming they took these photos in the middle of the night, when it was dark in the shop."

I was putting the pieces together. "And Iris had the camera, and Janice had every reason to try to get out of trouble for wrecking her parents' new car."

"Yep," Brenda agreed. "And those three just filled the banana-split boat with ice cream, added gumdrops, put a toothpick on top, set it in the glass display case to rotate like a UFO, and snapped the camera. Hoax accomplished."

Then Brenda wrinkled her brow. "But the big difference we have to overcome is that *their* picture gives the appearance of spinning, of moving, of rotating."

I nodded. "We don't have that rotating pie case," I concluded.

"Ah, but we *do*! For your scientific amusement tonight, dear Gen, we have the pièce de résistance," Brenda crowed.

She had obviously been working on this part for a long time.

She took a dinner plate and set it on some kind of pedestal-like tubular device that looked fashioned from parts rejected by a former anemometer project. Atop that contraption and the dinner plate Brenda set the banana-split saucer.

"Now, Mother," Brenda said, "you'll use this yardstick and plunk it right here"—she pointed—"right next to this closer end of the banana-split boat." Her mother obliged.

"Dad," she said, "you move around the boat and take lots of pictures from lots of different angles." Mr. Wompers nodded in agreement.

"Now, Gen," she said, "you'll do the counting as soon as the pedestal starts to move."

"Counting?"

"You know, your one thousand and one, one thousand and two routine."

"Ahh," I said.

"And you stop counting as soon as the banana-split boat has made one full circle, right? OK," Brenda announced. "Ready everybody?"

Then Brenda plugged in the cord, and the pedestal began to rotate. The dinner dish began to turn. The glass banana-split saucer began to orbit.

I began to count. But I could have predicted the outcome before the banana-split boat made one full circle. One thousand and twelve.

As her father snapped picture after picture from angle after angle, I marveled at the cleverness of Brenda Wompers.

When we had finished, Brenda said, "Now we just have to get these photos developed. I'm sure part three will be the most convincing part of my physics project presentation."

"Brenda," I suddenly blurted out, "are you *crazy*? You're not actually going to *present* all this at school, are you?" Now I was sure that Brenda and her family understood not a single thing about dealing with people.

Brenda looked at me in alarm. So did both her parents.

"How could I *not* present it, Gen?" she asked.

All three of the Womperses nodded their heads.

In my head echoed the Emily Dickinson poem we had read today in English class.

Tell all the Truth but tell it slant—
Success in Circuit lies
Too bright for our infirm Delight
The Truth's superb surprise;
As Lightning to the Children eased
With Explanation kind,
The Truth must dazzle gradually
Or every man be blind—

"Do you realize the *trouble* you're going to cause?" I offered weakly.

Brenda and her parents regarded me as an object of horror. "But Gen, dear," Mrs. Wompers said, "great scientists have *always* caused trouble."

I spent many afternoons at the lifeguard station working on the poems for Mr. Henderson's poetry notebook. There were poems about the conch and the hermit crab; poems about the fishing trawlers and the ocean liners; poems about the tidal pools and the jetties; poems about the boardwalk and the ocean shore.

Of late I'd been concentrating on a single poem. It had something to do with the red and green hemispheres and a high, wide fence running between them. I had learned that my poetry came most freely when I was alone and quiet, when I had settled into a place of calm. Only then did I have the freedom to listen.

Sometimes Brenda's visits seemed like an intrusion.

When Brenda appeared, she began tinkering with her gadgets and gauges, and I put away my poetry notebook. Still, I was delighted by the appearance of the lifeguard station, for it bore the hallmarks of our friendship. Colorful blobs of melted taffy pieces decorated the walls. Words like *antiestablishmentarian* and *Communist* scarred the wood. The ground below was littered with cigarette butts that Brenda had carefully arranged into a design with our initials: *G* and *B*. Every cranny of the station itself was crammed with gauges and gadgets that hung from the ceiling, fortified the walls, and rested along the floor. Brenda's latest project had been hooking up her gauges to whistles and bells; then when the wind blew, depending on its speed, a chorus of either gentle tinkling or loud chiming began to sing.

As Brenda's experiments chimed in my ears, I was reminded of the Edgar Allan Poe poem Mr. Henderson had read to us. "The Bells," like the lifeguard station, throbbed and hummed with the music of bells.

How they tinkle, tinkle, tinkle,
In the icy air of night!
While the stars that oversprinkle
All the heavens, seem to twinkle
With a crystalline delight.

"Brenda, you'd better think twice about presenting your ideas about Janice and Iris's flying saucer sighting. No, make that three or four times. You can't even *begin* to imagine what they'll do."

I remembered the ugly way those girls had campaigned against Sally. The worst thing had involved Wills. One of their campaign posters had gone up along the walls of the middle school. "LOOK WHO'S VOTING FOR SALLY REDMOND!" the sign read. Atop the words was an unflattering picture of Wills, caught when he was outside his locker struggling, as he always did, to remember the combination to his own lock. The way his ears stuck out and his teeth extended over his bottom lip had always made Wills look vulnerable to me; in the picture those characteristics simply made him look dumb. Thank goodness for Mrs. Rochelle, the physical education teacher, who had the posters taken down.

"Those girls will get hysterical," I said.

Brenda had been tinkering with some old metal spoons. "Science doesn't respond to hysteria," she sniffed. "It doesn't permit a blackmailing of the truth. Science remains cool and objective."

I watched as she drilled holes in the ends of her spoons. She planned to link the spoons together and then hang them from one of her gauges as another oddball addition to her collection of chimes.

What I had learned about Salem suggested that witchcraft flourished in a climate of insecurity. The community at Salem had been plagued with many threatening changes. There was the threat of Indian attack. There were the ravages of smallpox. There was the growing economic rivalry between Salem Village and Salem Town. There were newfangled religious ideas being bandied about. There were young girls undergoing puberty, whispering secretly about their changing sexuality in a climate of repression and superstition.

"Our school's not an environment where logic's likely to prevail," I said. The environment at Easton High School seemed every bit as insecure to me as the environment at Salem.

I thought back to my father's newspapers, to the *Weekly Reader* articles, to the televised Army-McCarthy trials, and to the Cold War that sent shivers of insecurity throughout the larger world. How different was Salem, Massachusetts, of 1692 from Easton, North Carolina, of 1954?

"They'll gossip about you, Brenda."

She shrugged and picked up a heavy set of leather harness bells fetched from a box in her parents' store. She planned to hook them to the base of her largest anemometer. "Gossip's simply the conversation of small minds," she said.

Hear the loud alarum bells—
Brazen bells!
What a tale of terror, now, their turbulency tells!

"They'll distort the truth." I had made a flowchart of the Salem Witch Trial accusations, attempting to trace the paths of the rumors like a kind of rocket trajectory. So far

I had paths leading from Elizabeth Parris and Abigail Williams to Sarah Good and Sarah Osborne. From there, the paths appeared to lead to Rebecca Nurse and Martha Corey and Elizabeth Proctor, but I wasn't exactly sure. Rumors and accusations didn't take a predictable path like an orbiting rocket. My chart had been filled with zigzags and arrows pointing in all directions.

"Scientific truth has always been fodder for rumors and distortions. And it's always been terrific at standing up to them."

"They'll call you names. Look at what they've done to Oppenheimer just this summer."

I knew about J. Robert Oppenheimer because of my father's incessant newspaper reading. My *Weekly Reader* had also reported on Oppenheimer, the world's most famous scientist other than Einstein. Oppenheimer had overseen the Manhattan Project, the secret effort during World War II to create the atomic bomb. But after the war, once he'd witnessed the destructive power of his own creation, he'd had reservations about going forward with Truman's plans for the hydrogen bomb. For those reservations he'd been suspected of being a traitor, and his security clearance had been revoked.

"What they did to Oppenheimer was right," Brenda declared.

"*Right*? Do you mean they were right to discredit

him?" Now Brenda sounded like my father and Senator McCarthy. "Just because he didn't want even more destructive scientific research to go forward?"

"It's impossible to halt the progress of science," she declared. "But beyond that, it's wrong to try to." She was finished with the sleigh bells now, and she slapped her hands in satisfaction.

I wasn't following her now. I wondered if perhaps she hadn't heard me. "Wait a second," I said. "Aren't you and your parents the ones who've been opposing the destructive power of the atom?"

"Be careful with your words, Gen. You're the wordsmith, remember." She turned the full seriousness of her dark brown eyes on me. Behind her eyes I could sense things revving, like a turbine. "Think about what you just said, Gen. 'The destructive power of the atom.'"

"So?"

"The atom itself is just an atom." She shrugged her shoulders. "It has no destructive power on its own. It's only the scientific development of it that makes it destructive."

"OK, OK," I said. I thought she was quibbling now.

"The development of the atom has to be placed in the most intelligent hands. In the hands of the scientists, of course. They'll know how best to develop it, how best to control it."

Her words stunned me. "But aren't scientists human, too? What guarantees do you have that scientists will use atomic power any more responsibly than politicians or even folks like you and me, Brenda?"

Brenda turned a pair of calm and objective eyes on me. "Those that understand science best are best able to make decisions about its use," she declared matter-of-factly.

My mind was in a whirl. There would be no more writing for me today. I could feel the pounding in my brain from the din of cowbells, sleigh bells, spoon bells, jingle bells. Like Poe, I believed the sound of those bells would drive me mad.

> *Keeping time, time, time,*
> *In a sort of Runic rhyme,*
> *To the tintinnabulation that so musically wells*
> *From the bells, bells, bells, bells,*
> *Bells, bells, bells—*
> *From the jingling and the tinkling of the bells.*

Still, I decided, if Brenda Wompers could have Rules for Thinking, so could Genevieve Hardcastle. In my heart I could yet believe this: "An idea is not necessarily true or false because it is discounted by another person."

25

Still, in spite of our differences, I knew how much Brenda needed me as a sounding board, and I couldn't blame her for wanting to talk. Lighting cigarette after cigarette, she recounted her frustrations. She had accompanied her parents to a Parent-Teacher Association meeting. After the members finished discussing their plans for the Halloween costume party and the idea of including parents for the first time this year, Mr. and Mrs. Wompers attempted to buttonhole parents as they left, trying to convince them to sign their petition. Both the parents and the teachers had walked away. The next day, Brenda had approached her classroom teachers, the ones who knew her personally, and had a bit more luck. Mrs. Pagano, Mr. Henderson, and Mr. Reuthven permitted her to display her mother's green brochures on their desks. But not a single student had reached out to take one. Finally, still determined to succeed, Brenda lit on another plan.

Outside her school locker, Brenda set up a makeshift campaign stand. I admired her resourcefulness. She had brought a folding, metal TV table from home and set it up between classes in the hallway. During each ten-minute break she would hurry to her locker and unfurl the petition dramatically. Carefully she laid the petition out across the tin surface of the table painted with a gaudy scene of cactus plants on a Western desert at sunrise. When she began her "step-right-up" campaign, urging her classmates to sign the petition, she sounded like a carnival barker for nuclear awareness. And whenever she set up her petition stand, Mr. Wrinkle, our principal, hovered nearby.

Brenda was elated that her between-class activities had encouraged a handful of signatures: some seniors with their sights set on Ivy League colleges; a few juniors who hoped to follow in their footsteps; and Isaac Beerbauer, a tenth-grader whose parents had been part of the effort to establish the state of Israel. Still, there was not a single signature from even one ninth-grader. Including me.

After Brenda's makeshift stand had been set up for several days, Mr. Henderson approached Brenda at her locker.

"Where's that famous Hollywood pen?" he asked. Usually I was offended by a teacher's corny attempt at humor. But not when the teacher was Mr. Henderson.

Brenda beamed. She passed him the Desilu Studios pen.

With a flourish Mr. Henderson signed his name to the petition. I recognized the familiar loopy *o*'s and *e*'s. It was the same hand that had made notations in a copy of *King Lear*, the same hand that had marked an A across a poem I had written. "There's my John Hancock," he quipped.

Then he paused and looked over the short list of signatures, nodding over a few he recognized. Mr. Henderson frowned and looked over at me. "I don't see your name there, Genevieve," he said. "I confess I'm a bit surprised."

I felt my face flush. I kept silent.

"Good work, Miss Wompers," he said, giving her a congratulatory wink. "It's about time we developed students around here who can think for themselves."

As I watched him return to his classroom, his leather elbow patches lurching as he jostled his way down the crowded hallway, I was overcome with guilt about my reluctance to sign. The truth was that I was afraid of identifying myself as even *more* of an outsider among my peers. And I was afraid of my parents' reaction should they find out. I worried: Where were my loyalties? To Brenda? To my family? To myself alone? To what I perceived as the truth?

26

We were preparing for November's confirmation ceremony in earnest now.

Reverend Steward had taken the class to the sanctuary for a practice rehearsal, and there was an electric excitement in the air.

During our practice session we lined up at the back of the church to practice marching, one by one, down the thick blue carpet. As I watched the other confirmands each take their solitary walk down the blue carpeted runway, I thought about how much I had always loved this sanctuary. The wooden pews were painted a crisp, pure trellis white, and the carpet ran up the middle like a flowering of blue morning glories. Most of all I loved the stained glass windows that circled the side walls like gem-colored portholes. Each of them showed Jesus at an important moment of his ministry: Jesus and the little children; Jesus and the loaves and the fishes; Jesus and the baptism of John; Jesus and the wedding at Cana.

When it was my turn, I felt nervous walking up the aisle alone while the others who had reached the front stood in a semicircle and stared at me. When I reminded myself that God was watching me from the huge wooden cross that hung above the altar, my confidence grew.

Afterward, when Wills had left for work and the other students had gone on their way, I hung behind.

Shyly, I asked Reverend Steward if I could speak to him.

He looked concerned.

I wondered if anyone my age had ever asked to speak with him before.

"Of course, Genevieve," he said. "Here, have a seat." He sat in the first row of white pews; I sat beside him.

"Well," I began. "It has something to do with what you said a few weeks ago about our neighbor and bearing false witness and all of that."

"I remember," he said.

"We were talking about the new girl. Brenda."

"Oh, yes," Reverend Steward said, grinning wryly, "the odd one with the funny sandals."

"Well," I said, encouraged by the laughter behind his words, "she's my best friend." I gulped.

"She's not exactly my 'best' friend. Sally Redmond's my best friend, only she moved away." I suddenly felt sheepish admitting this. "I guess Brenda's my *only* friend."

"I see," Reverend Steward said. "And your *only* friend

is somebody different, somebody odd. And even *you* can't quite claim her completely as your friend the way you had Sally Redmond. Is that right?"

"That's right." He made it sound simple, even though I knew it wasn't. "But there's more."

Reverend Steward waited.

"Brenda's parents are the ones you've been reading about in the newspaper. The ones who protested the Civil Defense program up at school. The ones who went before the school board. . . ."

"Let me finish for you," Reverend Steward said. "Let me guess." He paused. "And the ones everybody's calling Communists."

I felt a sense of pure relief.

"I recall that our conversation from the other week had something to do with bearing false witness. The ninth commandment. You must feel caught up in all this controversy somehow, Genevieve, if you're the only young person in Easton in contact with the Wompers family."

"I am. I do." The look in his eyes encouraged me to go on. "I've been troubled by those ideas about bearing false witness. People are accusing Brenda and her family of things that aren't true. They're not Communists, Reverend Steward. They're *not*."

His words were reassuring. "Perhaps we can both see more clearly why we're not supposed to bear false witness, why there's a commandment against it."

I thought it was kind for him to sweep me up into the embrace of his comments: *We. Both.*

"Do you feel like you're being falsely accused because you're Brenda's only friend? A kind of guilt by association?"

"Sort of. I haven't signed her petition, although I think I should. I've been thinking a lot about the Civil Defense program, and I'm coming to agree with Brenda and her parents. More accurate information needs to be given out. But I'm afraid, too." I paused to catch my breath. Then I went on. "I feel like a coward because I haven't signed that petition, and yet if I do, I'll be falsely accused of being a Communist. *For sure.*"

Reverend Steward's mouth turned down with a worried expression. "That's an awful lot for one young person to deal with," he acknowledged sympathetically. "What do your parents think about this, Genevieve?" he asked.

"I can't talk to my parents." I could feel the stinging behind my eyes; it was like opening my eyes to the salt when I swam in the ocean. "They hate the Wompers family. My parents think they're Communists, too. The only reason they let me have anything to do with Brenda is that she's tutoring me in algebra and we're working on a report together for school."

Reverend Steward frowned. He looked disappointed. Then he took a deep breath.

"Well, then," Reverend Steward asked, "How can I help? Or more to the point, how can your *faith* help you?"

I had been hoping *he* could answer that question for me.

Now the sanctuary dimmed. A cloud must have passed over the sun, for the gem-colored shards of glass in the stained glass windows grew darker.

"Wasn't Jesus faced with a similar problem?"

I was startled by his question. I had never thought of my problem in those terms. I remembered the way Jesus had been accused of being a false prophet and of wanting to be an earthly king. And He'd been betrayed by Judas, a person He considered His friend.

"How do you think Jesus handled it, Genevieve?"

"I'm sure He prayed," I offered.

"I think so, too," Reverend Steward confirmed. "When He was troubled, Jesus always prayed."

"But I've been doing that," I said. "It helps," I admitted. "But the problem is still there."

"Maybe prayer doesn't work like that," Reverend Steward offered. "Maybe prayer doesn't work like a magic wand. Maybe you don't just wave it around and then— *voilà!*—problem solved."

I watched him wave his steady hand in the air.

"Maybe prayer works mostly to help us listen better when we're troubled. To help us listen more reverently for what God wants us to do."

What Reverend Steward said made sense to me.

I let Reverend Steward's words wash around me like

the sounds of the ocean. Perhaps prayer was like the conch shell, something that helped us listen carefully until our heart finally heard an answer.

"And Jesus often advised us to turn the other cheek," Reverend Steward went on, *"to forgive those who trespass against us."*

Reflected in Reverend Steward's eyes was the shimmering image of my stricken face. "I'm not saying forgiveness is easy, Genevieve. It's not. I'm saying forgiveness might be part of the solution. After all, when the devil's forces are abroad in the world, they must somehow be put to rest."

The word struck me hard. *Devil.* It was a word that reminded me of a lot of other words. *Witch. Communist. Retard.*

I wondered aloud. "Reverend Steward, do you believe in the devil? I mean a real, living, breathing presence that causes evil in the world?"

"No doubt about it, Genevieve," Reverend Steward responded. "The Bible certainly mentions Satan. Remember when Jesus went out into the wilderness and the devil whispered in His ear, attempting to lead Him into temptation?" He pointed to the stained glass window on our left.

My eyes turned to the window across the sanctuary from us. It depicted a worried Jesus on his knees in prayer in the middle of a wilderness; a symbolic red ear trumpet represented the evil Satan whispering troubling words into Jesus' ear, and yet the Bible and the accusers at the Salem Witch Trials treated Satan as if he were real.

Reverend Steward ran his fingers through his short dark hair as if the gesture might clarify his thinking. "The important thing to me has not been to recognize an actual devil figure like a Satan, but to recognize evil as a presence in the world. And to be determined to defeat it."

I lingered over the image in the stained glass window. Jesus looked terribly alone.

"Isaiah says to refuse evil and choose the good."

I wondered aloud: "But how can you recognize the good in order to choose it?"

Reverend Steward leaned across the pew and lifted a Bible from the hymn rack. He flipped to the back of the Bible. "It's right here in Luke, Genevieve. The New Testament says goodness is like a tree: You recognize it by its fruits."

Now he slipped his index finger down the page, finding the passage he was seeking. "A good tree bringeth not forth corrupt fruit, neither doth a corrupt tree bring forth good fruit," he read. "For every tree is known by his own fruit."

I was getting confused.

"I understand about *corrupt* fruit," I said. "But I'm not sure what you have to do to produce the good fruit."

Reverend Steward closed the Bible and slipped it back into the hymn rack. "Maybe a fruit is not a *thing*."

I'm sure he read the confusion on my face.

He took another tack. "Let's take a simple noun. *Father,* for instance. *Father* is a noun, correct? A person, place, or thing, right?"

I nodded.

"But a true father can't be static or still. A true father is active—doing, producing. A true father is *fathering.* He's more like a verb than a noun. Does that make sense?"

I caught a glimmer of clarity.

"Maybe the 'fruit' Luke refers to is an action, a force, a behavior, a doing."

Reverend Steward was beginning to make sense to me. Perhaps the devil or witches weren't literal beings but *active forces,* like a verb. Perhaps a Communist wasn't so much the nounlike *thing* but the verblike way of *behaving* or *thinking* that frightened people.

I began to wonder about the forces inside me that could lead me in the direction of either goodness or corruption. As far as my association with Brenda, I hadn't yet produced anything: no allegiance to her petition, no signature on her paper. I hadn't come down either way: either for my friend or against her. I'd been a static, place-holding noun.

I wondered: Was *not doing something* a kind of "fruit"? I thought back to Mrs. Wompers and her comments to the school board: "The worst thing that can happen is if we allow ourselves to become apathetic."

I asked Reverend Steward one final question: "Can *in-*

action produce fruit? Can *doing nothing* be considered a verb?"

Reverend Steward pointed in the direction of another window. It was the window depicting Jesus with the loaves and the fishes, amply feeding a huge crowd with a small basket of meager offerings. "I think we've done enough hard thinking for one day, Genevieve. Let's remember that Jesus will feed us plentifully, especially when we find that our portion is small. We can talk again about this. It's not a problem to be solved in a day, is it? Let's pray about it, shall we?" he asked.

We bowed our heads, whispering the words of the Lord's Prayer.

27

don't know for sure what finally tipped the balance. But it might have been the love song.

"I hope you don't mind," Mr. Henderson said. He had sought me out in hallway 2B, just outside my biology class. "I hope I'm not intruding. But I was wondering if you might stop by my classroom after school."

"Sure," I said. I had learned that a visit to Mr. Henderson's classroom was always worth the effort.

He asked me to take a seat, and he then sat on top of his desk, his lanky legs swinging loosely over the edge.

"I got to thinking," he began, "that things can't be easy for you."

I was astonished. Mr. Henderson seemed to be able to read my thoughts. My heart melted with gratitude.

"I thought this might help," he continued, offering me a folded paper from a brown accordion file on the desk. "It's another poem. Most students don't think much of poetry. But you and I know they dismiss it too easily."

I felt a shiver at the back of my neck. *"You and I know."*

I glanced at the title on the paper. It was something about a love song. We'd been reading love poetry in class. We'd read love poems by Elizabeth Barrett Browning, by Christina Rossetti, by Percy Shelley, and by William Shakespeare. The author whose name appeared at the top of the page was T. S. Eliot.

"This is a challenging poem, Genevieve," Mr. Henderson said. "It's very modern. It's different from the love poems we've been discussing in class. Not every student would understand it," he said, running an index finger across the bristly mustache on his upper lip. "Perhaps you will."

"Thank you, sir," I stammered, flattered by his faith in me. "I'll try to figure it out," I said, "as best I can." I wanted him to know that although I liked poetry, I didn't claim to understand it.

"You don't really 'figure out' poems," he said, a wry smile beneath his warm brown mustache. "You just nudge out a little understanding a piece at a time."

Later, lying across my bed, I lost myself in the lines of Mr. Henderson's poem. "The Love Song of J. Alfred Prufrock," it was called. Mr. Henderson was right: it was different; it was challenging. But J. Alfred Prufrock seemed a person just like me: unsure, indecisive, unable to act.

And indeed there will be time . . .
To prepare a face to meet the faces that you meet;
Time for you and time for me,
And time yet for a hundred indecisions,
And for a hundred visions and revisions,
Before the taking of a toast and tea.

I understood all about the hundred indecisions and re-visions. They seemed like a nagging toothache: they were an ever-present part of my life now.

And indeed there will be time
To wonder, 'Do I dare?' and, 'Do I dare?'
Time to turn back and descend the stair,
With a bald spot in the middle of my hair.

As I read the poem carefully, over and over, I saw my-self like the attendant lord near the poem's end. I, unlike Brenda, was politic and cautious; I was one who stood by and merely deferred. Like J. Alfred Prufrock, I was hesi-tant and afraid.

Shall I part my hair behind? Do I dare to eat a peach?
I shall wear white flannel trousers, and walk upon the
    beach.
I have heard the mermaids singing, each to each.
I do not think that they will sing to me.

The "Love Song" and the challenges of this fall had taught me two things: Inaction was a verb, and I had been a bystander all my life.

I thought back to my girlhood and that time with Wills.

Wills was a few years older than me and the boys in the neighborhood, yet he always seemed younger than us. Perhaps it was his awkward, shuffling manner. But to me Wills had always seemed younger and more vulnerable because of his innocence. He didn't really understand why he was treated as different. He wanted to be just like the other boys. That was what the secret atomic decoder ring was all about.

The other boys, in fact, had started a club. The members would be only those boys who had one of those rings. Wills, therefore, assumed his ring entitled him to membership. That ring meant those boys would be his friends, that those boys would let him join their kickball games, their baseball teams, their swimming outings.

But Wills didn't and couldn't understand that those boys would never let him be part of their group. No matter what he owned or did or said.

"Why can't I play?" Wills asked when the other boys in the club started up a touch football game without him. Across his face was spread the wide-open prairie of his longing to belong. "I've got a ring, too, fellas."

Sally and I watched from a distance as Wills held up the ring.

We saw Link Palmer whistle to the other boys, and then they galloped toward Wills like a herd of buffalos.

"Is that so?" they jeered, surrounding Wills.

Link Palmer had given the other boys a sly wink. "We'll let you into the club if you'll do one thing."

"Sure, fellas," Wills said. The prairie of his face was blooming with sunlight.

"Show us your wiener."

Wills looked confused, like he did whenever he was called on in class.

"Your dick. Your goodies," Brad Connors said.

"Don't!" Sally cried. "Leave him alone!"

Now Wills's face darkened with the rain clouds of understanding.

"OK," he said. "Sure. You're my buddies, right?"

"Right," the boys, agreed, nodding their wicked heads.

And Wills took down his pants.

While the other boys laughed and pointed and rolled around on the ground, Wills's face spread with the pinkish red color of cornfields at sunset. "Can I play now, fellas?" He held the atomic secret decoder ring up to the light. "Am I in the club now?"

They were on him in an instant, but not before Wills wrenched his arm free and tossed the ring in my direction. I flung myself onto the ground and over the ring while I heard Sally yelling, "You better stop! I'm gonna tell!"

Now Brad Connors lunged at Sally. Even then, he was bigger and taller than the other boys his age. "If you tell, we'll get you, too."

I scrambled to my feet as Sally struggled to stand her ground.

I wanted to shriek, to yell, to cry for help, but I felt my tongue like a foreign object in my own mouth; I was so frightened I thought I might bite it off.

As Sally wrestled free from Brad Connors, she grabbed my hand, and we both tore off in the direction of home and safety. Words of protest lodged in my throat, but as I ran, I uttered only silent screams.

Afterward, Wills ran home crying, without his underpants and his play shorts.

Later, Aunt Minna questioned me. This was the same Aunt Minna who was kind and warm, who read to me in defiance of my father's scowls.

"What happened, Genevieve?"

I saw the swollen pillows under her eyes that meant she had been crying.

In my guilt I turned away from her and in the direction of Wills's face. That sweet face now seemed ravaged.

"Tell her, Gen," he pleaded.

I hung my head, lowering my eyelids over my eyes the way a hermit crab lowers the protective covering of a claw across his soft, vulnerable stomach. "I don't know," I lied. "I didn't see what happened."

28

After the school board meeting, my father redoubled his efforts on behalf of the pool. With rising hope, I had watched my father put away his maps and flags and shortwave radio; with rising determination, he had pored over advertisements for concrete and sent orders in to rental companies for surveying equipment and backhoes.

One afternoon when I returned from school, a backhoe snoozed in the backyard, and one morning a concrete truck appeared. The evenings were marked by the appearance of Uncle Bud and the surveying sticks and strings that marked off a wide rectangle across our backyard. Each night as they finished their work, my father and my uncle left a shovel standing at attention in the ground.

For my part, I tried to ensure the success of the pool project by keeping a close eye on my mother. I knew that if she nosed around talking too much or asking too many questions, my father might change his mind and abandon the project altogether. I had developed a routine for handling her on those occasions: I quickly pulled her aside, dragging her by the elbow into the house.

"Mother," I asked, "do you think the red in my sweater matches the red in this skirt? Aren't they two different shades?"

After that, I knew what she'd do: She'd step back, study me, and then frown. "Well, as a matter of fact, Genevieve, I believe you're right. Those shades just don't *go*, sweetie."

"Then, Mother," I pleaded, proud of my ability to divert her attention, "would you look in the drawer with me and help me find a better match?"

As we peered into the rectangle of dresser drawer, relief flooded my body. Perhaps someday a swim might not require a secret five-mile pedal to the beach.

I had finally signed Brenda's petition, and ever since, I'd struggled to account for my courage. Perhaps it wasn't one thing. Perhaps it was a combination of Janice Neddeger and the Salem project and Reverend Steward's conversation and my experiences with my cousin Wills and my friendship with Brenda and the unyielding fears in my own heart and J. Alfred Prufrock. Everything all at once.

The afternoon after I had signed the petition, Brenda appeared suddenly over a dune with a box of fried chicken from a stand on the boardwalk.

"I always knew he was ridiculous," she scoffed, referring to the Civil Defense officer and his program that day, "but this time even Eddie Brinkley could be heard guffawing in the back of the classroom."

I remembered. The Civil Defense lesson had presented especially preposterous advice. But I had wondered: Was it the lesson that had changed or was it I that had changed? Was there something in me that was now able to hear the old lesson in a new way? Was it true what Reverend Steward had said? That you had to learn to listen before you could really hear?

Now Brenda mimicked the Civil Defense officer's lesson. She screwed up her face, turning it into that of a haughty Englishwoman: "You can survive an atomic attack by sending your children," she said, her nose high in the air, her voice nasal and squeaking, "to the country."

Then she jumped from the railing of the lifeguard shelter onto the hot sand below. She danced about on the hot white powder like Bridey Murphy doing a jig. "Don't be alarmed that the coins in your pocket," she said, hopping from one foot to the other, "will become temporarily heated."

Now Brenda leaped up the steps to the lifeguard shelter two at a time. "Keep your car windows rolled up," she warned me, shaking her fingers in my face.

"Wear your hat brim down to prevent face burns," Brenda advised, stuffing the fat end of another drumstick into her mouth.

Then she added, "Remember to stockpile essential items," Brenda warned. "Like sheets and pillowcases."

Now I joined in the comedy. "Or a lantern," I offered, picking up the theme.

"Or a bottle of sodium bicarbonate."

"And a can opener with plenty of canned goods."

"And, oh, yes," Brenda added, "most important would be a pint of whiskey!"

As I watched my friend bent double with laughter, I recalled the moment I had signed the petition. It had been outside Brenda's locker in the hallway right before lunch.

The Hollywood pen had felt surprisingly light in my hand, and my signature had scrawled itself easily across the page. After I had signed, I felt lighter, somehow.

Afterward, Brenda had merely said, "I knew you just needed time, Gen. Some people are like that." As she had put away her stand to go to her next class, she had added, "Thanks. I knew I could count on you."

Now, at the lifeguard station, I acknowledged that there was one thing about Brenda Wompers I admired most of all. It wasn't her fascination with science or her patience with my algebra studies or her acceptance that I needed time to make decisions or her faith that I could be counted on. Looking at her devouring chicken and mocking the Civil Defense officer, her curls as wobbly and womperjawed as her name, I decided that I loved Brenda Wompers because she was nothing like Janice Neddeger and the other girls. She was an original, one of a kind.

29

It was clear that the Womperses' business was failing. The western paperbacks and romance novels had been replaced by academic books of only regional interest. They bore titles like *Crustaceans of the Tidal Pools; The Sea Grasses: A Study in Variety Amidst Simplicity; The Stormy Coast: Changes in the Coastal Shoreline of North Carolina in the Early 20th Century.* Only the occasional visiting professor now perused the bookshelves or made a purchase.

Even the thrift store goods, a reliable staple of their business, failed to turn a profit. At every turn, Mr. and Mrs. Wompers gave away more clothing than they charged for. If a little girl entered the store with a pair of worn sandals, she was immediately treated to a pair of sturdy used ones. If a housewife came looking for a new skirt, she left with the skirt and the added bonus of some free new cereal bowls. If a boardwalk worker had a sick family member, that was all the more reason why the winter coats were free that day.

But I was alarmed by what Mrs. Wompers did with the conchs. The conch shells, like the natural treasure I held to my ear at night, were one of the store's most popular items. Every tourist on Easton Beach was eager to return home with a conch shell as a memento of their stroll along the Carolina coast. But Mrs. Wompers had been consulting a scientific catalog that declared those conchs inauthentic. She discovered that the conchs sold in her shop were not native to our eastern shore but were native instead to the Florida coast. She determined to weed them from the shop.

"We can't in good conscience, Harry," I overheard her telling Mr. Wompers, "sell those items as representative of this region. It would perpetuate a fraud on our customers."

Mr. Wompers considered what his wife said. "Yes, I suppose you're right, dear. Our shop is striving after authentic Carolina merchandise. Selling Florida conchs as Carolina conchs surely compromises that integrity."

I was astonished. I loved my conch. I didn't care whether my conch was from the Florida coast or from Timbuktu.

"I think," I spoke up, "that most of your customers won't care where the conchs come from. I think you can be satisfied by offering them something from nature that can be admired. I don't think shoppers will care about the shore on which they've washed up."

"But *we* care, dear," Mr. Wompers said. "No, I think Trish is right. We just won't order any more of the conchs."

"Yes, Harry," Mrs. Wompers agreed. "But since you appreciate them so much," she said, turning her kittenish face to me and brightening, "we'll just give the rest of the supply to you, Gen."

Suddenly I was the proud owner of several dozen conch shells.

Sometimes, however, I thought the souvenir shop now belonged more appropriately on the carnival grounds. Alongside the arcade, perhaps. Beside the booths of the carnival barkers. Under the Womperses' ownership the souvenir store had become not the popular tourist haven of Raymond Donner's boardwalk days but a kind of curiosity shop, where the odd or the eccentric could feel free to wander without purchasing anything. Since the controversy over the Civil Defense program had lost them customers, I shuddered at the thought of Brenda's UFO presentation; it was likely to stir up the kind of anger that would surely ruin her parents' business. I regarded the Wompers family as smart and kind and interesting, but they, like their shop, often seemed like curiosities to me.

Because I still worried about the Wompers family even as I continued to grow frustrated with them, I held my ground about the saltwater taffy. There wasn't another store along the boardwalk that sold the multicolored sweets, and rare was the vacationer who could leave the shore without buying a bag to enjoy in the car on the ride home or to send to a distant relative or friend. A bag of saltwater taffy was as much a part of a beach vacation as a postcard of Easton Beach. Without the coconut patties or the conchs, shoppers who entered in hopes of purchasing a cheap trinket or even cheaper taffy would leave disappointed. In the back-and-forth debates that characterized conversation with the Womperses, I lobbied for the taffy's continued presence in the store; I hoped it would salvage some steady business for them.

With relief I learned that I'd finally persuaded them.

In fact, from time to time, after I'd finished work on my algebra problems with Brenda, Mr. and Mrs. Wompers and Brenda and I would sit at a card table and bag up the taffy for the shop.

We set up the taffy-bagging in a kind of makeshift assembly line. Mr. Wompers held open the plastic bags while Mrs. Wompers counted out twenty-four pieces of taffy. After she slipped them into the bag, she passed the bag to Brenda, who scissored off a length of colored ribbon. Then Brenda passed the ribbon to me, and I tied the taffy bags shut with a ribbon and slapped a label on the bag.

"Thanks, Genevieve," Mr. Wompers said, "for signing our petition."

"We're hopeful we can make some real progress on the issue now," added his wife.

"Yes," chimed in Brenda. "Gen's signing gave a couple more people the courage to sign. Maybe she's helped launch a trend."

I stared at the ribbon in my hand, wondering how the signatures of Wilma Turner and Eddie Brinkley could be considered a trend.

"They said," Brenda continued, "that they had always respected you and Sally. They didn't like the way the election was conducted last spring, and they wanted to show some support."

I'd never known that Sally and I might have been objects of respect. But I was glad a few more people had become verbs, not nouns. I knew how hard that transformation could be.

Mrs. Wompers reached for a cigarette and then passed the packet to her daughter. As *The Perry Como Show* played on the TV in the background, Mrs. Wompers lit her cigarette and her daughter's from a single match.

"By the way," I said, watching Brenda inhale and hoping that a person regarded with the respect that inspired two signatures might put forth a difficult opinion, "my father read me a newspaper article about smoking. There's a new study out. It says that smoking causes lung cancer. I've saved the clipping if you'd like to read it."

Brenda looked away from me and exhaled. "Hmm," was all she said. It was the same phrase my mother whispered when she half listened to my father's newspaper commentaries.

Then her mother tapped a long ash into the ashtray. The ash fell into the cavern between the two breasts of a naked ceramic lady lounging on Easton Beach. "Only a single study?"

"Yes," I added, "but they were saying it was an important one. And there was something about it in our *Weekly Readers*, too," I added, recalling the graphs and charts in the sidebar of the classroom newsmagazine. "The tobacco industry is going to be conducting one of its own studies, too. But that's not likely to be as trustworthy, given their interest in keeping people addicted to cigarettes."

"*Addicted?*" queried Brenda. "And how did the study define *addiction*?"

"Good point, dear," agreed her mother.

"Well, *I'm* not addicted to these things," Brenda insisted, taking one last drag and then stubbing her cigarette out. "*See?*"

I doubted Brenda's certainty. I figured she smoked about a pack a day.

"Well, dear," Mrs. Wompers said, turning her head and addressing me patronizingly, "one study's hardly conclusive."

As she exhaled, the smoke that drifted my way tingled my nostrils. I turned and waved the smoke away. Silently I added a Rule for Thinking to a secret list of my own:

People hold fast to their beliefs, even if those beliefs are contradicted by facts.

Brenda snipped off a length of pale green ribbon. "They ought to call it *The Perry* Comatose *Show*," she said, grinning.

I grinned back, slipping the green ribbon around the neck of a saltwater taffy bag.

"By the way, Gen," Mrs. Wompers began, finished with counting another series of twenty-four candies. "I'm curious about some of your religious beliefs. Specifically, I'm wondering whether your religion thinks of God as a man or a woman."

I lost my grasp on the loop I was making. *"Your religion."* Mrs. Wompers was like Brenda: She had a way of suddenly asking the most disconcerting questions at the most unexpected times.

Mrs. Wompers must have sensed my discomfort. "I hope you don't mind my asking, Genevieve. I was just curious and all. After talking to your Aunt Minna the other day."

I found myself tongue-tied. "No, sure," I stammered. "That's all right." I tried to recall the answers to the questions I had memorized in my confirmation class. There had never been a single word about whether God was a man or a woman. My mind drew a blank. "I guess I don't know," I confessed.

"Well, then," Brenda asked, "when you hold your hand over your heart to say the Pledge, preparing to say 'one nation, *under God*, indivisible,' how do you picture that 'God'?"

"I'm not sure I *can* 'picture' God," I replied. "Just like I can't picture the wind. It's just there. I feel it. I don't have a 'picture.'"

"Well, then, if you can't picture God, how would you *define* God?"

I thought back to the first day of school. This fall had been the first ever in which there had been changes in the wording of the Pledge of Allegiance I'd been reciting since childhood.

At the breakfast table last summer, my father had read aloud from the newspaper about it. "Eisenhower has finally signed that bill from Congress. Good for him. They've added 'under God' to the Pledge of Allegiance. That's one of the best things to happen in years. It's a punch in the stomach to godless Communists the world over."

I thought it was a good thing, too. I loved the God I prayed to. When I recited the Pledge, the words *under God* were my favorite part. Saying them sometimes gave me goosebumps.

Now, wondering how to answer Brenda's question, I studied the picture on the label of the taffy bag. It showed a lighthouse, a shoreline, and the sea. "I've thought about that sort of thing lots of times, Brenda," I said more confidently. "But it's hard to define God. God encompasses so much."

I scanned the clear and simple words on the label in my hand: *Saltwater. Taffy. Easton. North. Carolina.* The meanings of those words were clear.

I looked around at Brenda's mother and father. They had stopped work to look at me.

I thought back to the first day of Mr. Henderson's class when I had tried to define poetry. Like poetry, God was mysterious. "It seems like once you pin a definition on God, you've narrowed God already. Do you know what I mean?" I said, thinking out loud.

Brenda nodded.

"I guess," I said, "I've thought of God as love, perhaps. Or goodness." As I began speaking, my thoughts assembled themselves. It was sort of like writing my poems. "Yes, I guess I think of God as goodness. As all good."

The room was quiet for a moment as all of them looked at me.

"But if God is all good, Gen," Mr. Wompers asked thoughtfully, "how do you explain the badness in the world? Like war? Or ax murderers?"

"Or children with cancer?" added Mrs. Wompers. I noticed that a cigarette ash had just streaked down the front of her pink bathrobe.

"Or radiation poisoning?" added Mr. Wompers.

"Or Janice Neddeger?" added Brenda with a wobbly grin.

In the silence that followed, we picked up our taffy bagging again.

"Maybe," I offered, still struggling with my definition of God, "God is more than all goodness. Maybe God is all power." That seemed a reasonable definition. "Yes, I think that's closer to the truth. God is all-powerful."

Mrs. Wompers stubbed out her cigarette.

"But if God is all-powerful, dear," Mrs. Wompers said, grinding the butt end of her cigarette on the ceramic rump of the woman on the ashtray, "why does He allow a Hitler to come to power?"

"Why does He permit the destruction of hurricanes and earthquakes?" added Mr. Wompers.

Brenda's glasses had slipped down on her nose. Her dark brown eyes looked out at me from over the rim. "And why would an all-powerful God allow the hanging of innocent people as witches?"

Now Brenda's face was as sober as I had ever seen it. There was not a trace of the clownish womperishness that made up a large part of her character. "And if God isn't all-powerful—or all good—by logical extension, what is God's *point*?"

I could feel the anger burning hot inside of me. Suddenly the answer came all in a rush. "Brenda, God doesn't have to have a *point*. God just *is*. You don't have to define Him. He's everywhere. All around."

The Womperses stared at me, blinking absently as I went on. "God is awe and majesty and mystery. He's there in the conch's spiral. He's there in poetry and in the ocean's waves and in the impulse that wants us to think of each other as neighbors all, that wants us to bring forth good fruit, not corrupt."

The Womperses looked from one to the other, their blinking eyes as dull and unseeing as the black pinhead eyes of birds.

Mr. Wompers was the first to break the silence. "But that's not the kind of thinking we admire, Genevieve," he said, a touch of pity in his voice. "We can certainly appreciate all those things you mentioned, but they don't account for the existence of God," he said simply. "That's why we're atheists."

I saw the light glinting off his glasses like the swift silver flash of fish in the ocean, and I wondered if atheists could truly appreciate the staggering beauty of God's creation.

"Yes, dear," his wife explained, "we don't think it's rational to believe in God. Such belief makes no logical sense."

I saw the halo of light around Mrs. Wompers's gray hair and thought of the dappled leaves in a forest, backlit by streams of filtered light. I wondered if atheists could explain the source of that illumination.

"And my mother and father are going to be heading up to school again," said Brenda. "They don't think people should have to recite the words *under God* in the Pledge of Allegiance." Brenda's voice was ardent, fervent. "They're going to be launching a campaign of protest."

I felt the air sucked out of me. Once again, everything was womperjawed.

30

Brenda and I had stopped speaking.

We'd had an argument in the lunchroom, an argument followed by days of silence.

The argument had been mostly my fault. I had disparaged her lunch. Why was it, I wondered, that friendships fractured over such tiny things? After all, Brenda had been merely munching on a dry cracker spread with bean paste for the main course and a limp celery stick for dessert. Her bland and unappealing lunch was nothing out of the ordinary. Why, then, did noticing it finally send me into such a rage?

But the tension had been building for days.

In fact, sometimes I wasn't sure Brenda really listened to me.

Just the other day, as we strolled the boardwalk, Brenda smoked and gazed off into the ocean while I tried to explain once again that even the most airtight lineup of facts in the world wouldn't convince people that Janice and Iris faked that flying saucer photograph.

"That's ridiculous, Gen," Brenda insisted. "People know a fact when they see it. People respect evidence."

"All kinds of things pass for evidence, Brenda," I said. "Don't you remember about the spectral evidence presented at Salem?"

Brenda knew as well as I did that people in Salem believed in something called spectral evidence. Accusers could offer sightings of witches and demons before the judges, providing "evidence" of invisible specters in court at will.

"Easton High School will be just like Salem, Massachusetts, Brenda. Your facts won't make any difference. Most people will be swearing to their belief in flying saucers, and you—alone—will be swearing against it."

"We'll see."

"It's like you said yourself, Brenda. Seeing is not necessarily believing. People see what they want to see, hear what they want to hear, believe what they want to believe."

But on that day in the lunchroom the tension between us exploded.

"I shouldn't have to recite those words in the Pledge," Brenda insisted. "I shouldn't be forced to say things I don't believe in."

"But how do you know you don't believe in them? You and your parents admitted that you've never really gone to church or explored religion for yourselves." Something inside me was gathering power as I spoke. "Doesn't what you just said fly in the face of all your scientific attitudes?"

"Hmmmph," Brenda scoffed. "Religion's hardly a fit subject for scientific experimentation." She snorted. "Those words in the Pledge violate the Constitution. *Under God* clearly violates the amendment separating church and state."

"I don't see how you can quibble so much over two little words," I insisted.

A look of glee flooded her face as if Brenda the fox had just trapped Genevieve the chicken. "*You* would deride *quibbling over words*? The poet thinks 'two little words' are *unimportant*?"

She had me there. I gulped, swallowing a melon slice.

"Well, then," I offered, "just don't say them. No one's forcing you to."

"That's hypocritical," Brenda insisted. "If the words are inappropriate, they need to come out. Besides, it's shameful to be the only one who has to hold my tongue. It singles me out."

I threw back my head and laughed, almost choking on another melon slice. "Brenda Wompers doesn't like to be *singled out*?" Wasn't Brenda's whole being devoted to being different, to wearing different clothing, to thinking different thoughts?

I saw the black thundercloud cross her face. Brenda was getting angry.

I passed her an apple slice and tried to pacify her with another perspective. "It's not that big a deal, Brenda."

Brenda shoved my apple offering away from her. "There!" she exulted. "You've finally admitted it yourself, Gen. God isn't a big deal."

Now I found the storm cloud moving in my own direction as Brenda hurled her bolts of lightning. "If God's *not* such a big deal, why not just throw Him out of the Pledge altogether?"

That's when I had taken such disgusted notice of Brenda's luncheon fare. The stale cracker. The bean paste. The limp celery stalk.

As I watched her eat, I concluded that atheists were so odd they even ate food different from the rest of us. I blurted out, "Can an atheist, Brenda, appreciate the salty bite of a pickle or the syrupy rush of a peach's juice?"

"That's a ridiculous question," she declared, and she stomped off.

What she shouted before she stormed out of the lunchroom entirely were these words: "I *am* going to present that physics experiment, Gen Hardcastle. And nothing you can say will be able to stop me."

31

If it hadn't been for Mrs. Pagano and our scheduled conference, Brenda and I might never have spoken again. Since the Salem Witch Trials reports were due in only two weeks, Mrs. Pagano required all the students to meet with her.

On our appointed afternoon Brenda pulled up a chair and sat on the far right of Mrs. Pagano's desk. I pulled up a chair and sat on the far left.

Mrs. Pagano's bangle bracelets jingled at her wrists as she stretched her arms across her teacher's desk. Then she linked the fingers of her hand. "Have you decided on a hypothesis yet, ladies?"

Brenda and I had discussed a hypothesis for the report a number of times in the weeks when we were still speaking. A hypothesis was a kind of working theory, a point you hoped to prove.

Naturally, Brenda loved hypotheses. At the beach, she had enthused about hypotheses the way she'd been ecstatic about anemometers.

"Hypotheses are so *logical*, Gen," she'd exulted. "Hypotheses keep things simple."

I was not ecstatic about logic. Logic worked well in the world of math and science, perhaps. It didn't seem to work so well in the world of language. I knew from creating my poetry that poems possessed a kind of logic, but it wasn't the kind of XYZ logic Brenda made use of. Poetry seemed more to me like stumbling about blindfolded in a darkened room or like a mixed-up jumble in a sack from which you pulled things randomly. Its results, unique and unverifiable, arose from the connective streams of serendipity, association, intuition.

Icily Brenda hissed, "We think, obviously, that *science* can explain what happened at Salem."

I sighed. I didn't like being included in Brenda's "we." I'd come to believe that what happened at Salem defied the logic that Brenda so revered.

"No," I said firmly, noticing the chill in my own voice. "Not '*we*.' *You*."

I also resented Brenda's use of another word: *obviously*. It was a word related to *never* and *always*. It left out the possibilities of Reverend Steward's *maybe*.

"And not '*obviously*,'" I added.

I had learned a great deal about hysteria, rumors, gossip, the seventeenth-century definitions of *witch*, the cultural changes occurring in Salem, and other aspects of the black drama that had been played out there. How you could stuff it all into a single hypothesis, and a scientific one at that, wasn't so obvious.

Mrs. Pagano shifted in her seat. The stacks of journals on her desks wobbled. She cleared her throat. "I see. So our researchers have a difference of opinion," she said calmly. She turned to Brenda. "Can you give me a bit more detail about how *you* envision your working hypothesis, Miss Wompers?"

"Sure," Brenda said, glaring at me in triumph. I could read Brenda's conclusion on her gloating face: Mrs. Pagano had sought further explanation from her because our teacher believed Brenda's hypothesis was the more compelling one. "Scientists have produced some very persuasive evidence to explain what happened in Salem. They always do," Brenda sniffed, her sniff aimed directly at me.

"Some scientists think there might have been something in the air or the food in Salem to explain the hysteria," Brenda went on. "The most prominent of them think the hysteria might have been caused by ergot exposure."

Of late, Brenda had been fixated on the idea of ergot exposure. Frankly, I was tired of hearing about it. Brenda had learned that ergot is an herb that affects the ability to reason clearly. "The latest thinking is that the wheat fields around Salem harbored ergot," she said. "Poisoning. That's a plausible scientific explanation."

"Your turn, Genevieve," Mrs. Pagano said. "From what

you've said, I'm assuming you disagree with your partner. Is that right?"

I nodded and brought out the thick notebook I'd assembled. I'd done most of the writing and note-taking for the project, dividing our information up into notebook sections with different labels: SUPERSTITIONS IN SALEM, RELIGION IN SALEM, THE LEGAL SYSTEM IN SALEM, EXPLANATIONS FOR THE ACCUSATIONS. We'd collected facts about the judges for the trial like Jonathan Corwin and Captain Samuel Sewell; about the religious leaders of the time like Cotton Mather; about Tituba, the West Indian woman who may have influenced the afflicted girls' behavior.

"I'm not sure the evidence points to a scientific explanation," I began, flipping through some of the notebook pages, searching for the section I'd been most interested in.

"I've been collecting some information about the accusers, putting things together into a few charts here." I'd made detailed lists of the accusers' names: Anne Williams, Mary Warren, Mercy Lewis, and others. I'd also cataloged their age, social class, religious beliefs, and economic position in the community. I'd devoted one page to a description of each of the accusers at Salem.

Mrs. Pagano bent toward me for a closer look. "Interesting angle," Mrs. Pagano nodded. "It's kind of a sociological or psychological approach, isn't it? Like a series of case studies?"

Out of the corner of my eye, I could glimpse the angry points of Brenda's shoulders.

"Yes, I suppose it is," I nodded.

"So you explain the events at Salem from more of a human perspective? You're finding the causes, Genevieve, in human nature or human behavior itself, somehow?"

I nodded again. "Yes," I said tentatively. "I think so."

Now Brenda objected, interrupting me. "But you've not offered any *proof,* Genevieve. Sociology isn't really scientific. The explanations you've offered can't be repeated or verified."

Now Mrs. Pagano pursed her lips and raised her eyebrows in a gesture that forwarded Brenda's objections on to me. "And how do you respond to what your partner just said, Miss Hardcastle?"

Mrs. Pagano had given me an audience. But an audience was something that Brenda thrived on, not me. I felt breathless with anger and frustration. Unlike scientific truths, my truths couldn't be repeated or verified. Yet they were truths to me nonetheless.

To me, Brenda's way of thinking, the scientific way, was clearer, but its problems often seemed easier. It had tools like cyclotrons and calculators, unlike poetry, which had only words, words that attempted to make sense of things that seemed blurred and fuzzy. Science measured the readiness of the bread with thermometers; poetry poked at it with an index finger.

Floundering, I blurted, "Well, maybe my conclusions can't be repeated or verified as accurately as science would like," I said. "But to me it seems easier to rig up a banana-split boat and top it with a toothpick," I declared fiercely, "than to pin down the motivations of the human heart."

Suddenly Brenda's back arched. She thrust out her chin. She was furious. "Well," she shouted, "at least an experiment can tell you something conclusive."

A look of confusion spread across Mrs. Pagano's face. "Banana-split boat? Toothpick?" she asked. "Have we drifted from the subject of Salem, ladies?"

"No," I replied, determined to follow the trajectory of Brenda's objection. "Salem is exactly on point, Mrs. Pagano."

Now I stood up and faced Brenda, who had turned an icy profile to me. "Brenda," I protested, "haven't you gotten anything from the reading we've done about Salem? Don't you see evidence everywhere of the human tendency to factions and cliques, to whisperings and rumors, to control and power, even to death and destruction?"

"Those aren't scientific questions, Genevieve," she sniffed.

Brenda had folded her arms and completely turned her back to me.

I was stunned.

"Girls," Mrs. Pagano interjected. "Let's keep this discussion civil. Brenda," she said firmly, "turn around and listen to Genevieve."

I was astonished when Brenda turned back around. Antiestablishmentarians usually did just the opposite of what any authority figure requested.

"It seems to me, Brenda," I went on, "that whether it's simple colonists in gray Puritan garb or complicated thinkers in white lab jackets, death and destruction arise from human nature, human nature itself."

"Brenda," I began again, so caught up in what I was saying that I forgot about Mrs. Pagano, "have you forgotten the story of the scorpion and the frog?"

"Huh?"

Mrs. Pagano wrinkled her brow, too.

"The scorpion. And the frog. You know, that story you told me. About the scorpion that rides on the frog's back and stings him. Because it's in his nature."

Finally Brenda stood up to face me. The straight line of her glasses seemed a punishing rod. "That's an anecdote, Gen. It makes a point. But it's not science."

Now Mrs. Pagano thrust her voice between us in an attempt to break up our fight. "Girls," she insisted firmly, "listen, now. You're partners in this effort. You need to listen more carefully to what each of you has to say."

But Brenda couldn't stop talking. "Science and mathematics will ultimately explain everything, Gen. The pattern of a leopard's spots or a zebra's stripes. The spiral patterns of the conch. One day mathematics will even explain what happened at Salem. Until then, the priests and the sociologists and the poets can offer only jury-rigged explanations."

Brenda was rambling on. She was not listening.

Mrs. Pagano finally held up both arms, and the bracelets at her wrists hissed like the warning rattles of a snake poised to strike. "Young ladies," Mrs. Pagano insisted, laying one braceleted hand on Brenda's arm and the other hand on mine, "I'm assuming that this argument between you is about something else. Something other than your Salem report."

I nodded, and Brenda thrust out her bottom lip. Mrs. Pagano was almost right. The argument was about something other than Salem. Yet it was oddly about Salem, too.

"Perhaps I can suggest something," Mrs. Pagano interjected. "Perhaps I can suggest another way of thinking about this."

I could see that Brenda wasn't listening to our teacher.

"Perhaps what you're searching for, young ladies," she said helpfully, "isn't an either/or approach to the problem. Perhaps it's not one thing or the other. Perhaps it's not science *or* sociology. Perhaps it's both/and."

As I thought about what Mrs. Pagano said, I believed I understood it. It wasn't Brenda's ideas on one side and mine on the other. It wasn't either/or. It wasn't science against human nature. It was, perhaps, as Mrs. Pagano said, 'both/and.' It wasn't just one part of things; it was the whole of everything. But Brenda hadn't heard Mrs. Pagano because she wasn't listening. She had entered that world where only she and her parents could go.

32

was angry with Brenda, but I was furious with my father. I dived into the tossing surf, parting the waves with my arms as I thrust forward like the bow of a ship. The ocean today was churning with an anger that mimicked my own. I had rushed to the shore longing, as always, for the lightness of the waves that lifted me into their arms. But the undertow was strong today. Finally tired of wrestling with the water, I threw myself on the sand and closed my eyes.

I'd been disappointed in my father before. More than disappointed, actually. Embarrassed. Ashamed. I knew what the commandment said: *Honor thy father and mother.* But now I had to admit what my conversation with Reverend Steward had helped me see: My father knew nothing about fathering.

While the sand chafed my back I thought back to Career Day last spring. My father had been one of only several parents asked to make a short formal presentation to our class. I had been anxious about his appearance, and as each parent's presentation grew more interesting than the one before, my anxiety had turned to dread. Robbie Scoggins's father, a baker, had told the class about rising at four every morning to start the bread. He had passed out fresh elephant ears and a coupon for a free cookie. Marion Ramsey's mother, a nurse, had taught the class how to take a blood pressure reading with a blood pressure cuff. Just before recess, Charlie Luckett's father had spoken. Charlie's father was a firefighter, and he had brought red plastic helmets for every member of the class and had allowed them to climb all over the fire truck during recess.

After recess, it had been my father's turn. As my classmates had flung themselves into their seats, chattering about the fire truck, I had slid down in my seat. With apprehension, I had watched my father set his bland charts and diagrams on easels at the front of the class. He had announced to the class that he was in the "actuarial business." Even after his explanation, the students hadn't understood what an actuary was, exactly, but they knew George Hardcastle's job had to do with facts. It was important, he had announced to the class, to "stare facts in the face."

After he had picked up the pointer to explain the peak on a chart about soaring hospital admissions during the winter months, I had watched my classmates. They had been fidgeting with their pencils, passing notes behind their backs, and snoozing over their notebooks.

That night, over supper, my father had complained about the despicable behavior of the younger generation these days.

Now, however, my fury with my father was dark and irretrievable.

My parents had been arguing in the backyard. I was curious, for they rarely shouted. As I approached them I observed the glumness on my father's face as he stared into the backyard ditch that had been carved out for the swimming pool. I noticed the stiffness in my mother's lips when she spoke.

"Tell her, George," my mother commanded.

"What?" I asked. "Tell me *what?*"

My father stared into the huge hole in the backyard dug by the backhoe. Mounds of dirt were piled up along the edges.

I looked into my mother's face. Something was gathering there, like a burst of steam when you lifted the lid on a simmering pot. "You let us *believe*," she seethed, "that you were building us a pool."

As she spoke, my father's eyes turned back to me, squinting into the glaring sunlight, looking at me but not really seeing. "I don't control what you believe, Martha," he snapped back.

I was thoroughly confused. I had daydreamed about the swimming party at which I shared the pool with the other girls in their two-piece swimsuits. The daydreams had been filled with the sound of splashing water and the smell of baby oil.

And then my mother stepped over to me, linking her arm through mine. "And you let me go on thinking about installing a barbecue, George." It was not a statement but an accusation. "And then you let me run on about one of those big, round picnic tables with an umbrella in the middle to keep out the sun."

"You run on of your own accord, Martha."

I thought of a ballerina atop a music box. My father was right.

"And then, George," my mother chattered on, "you listened to me make all those plans about inviting the neighbors over and serving them lemonade in frosted glasses with those little cocktail umbrellas in them."

"You can make all the plans you like, Martha. I don't have to make them come true."

That night we ate a silent supper. The only sound was the clank of forks across plates, the thump of bowls picked up and put down.

I stared at the chicken and cauliflower on my plate. I suddenly recalled the Civil Defense officer and one of his lectures: A nuclear bomb could produce heat five times that of the interior of the sun. Now the chicken on my plate tasted like something charred beyond recognition. And I avoided the cauliflower altogether. With its broad billowy cloud atop its narrow stalk, it looked to me like a miniature nuclear cloud.

"Worst of all," my mother began, "was the way you've disappointed your daughter. We had plans for Gen to make some friends, finally, George. The closest thing she has to a friend is the daughter of those Communists. A teenage girl needs friends. A pool would have helped with that."

My mother's words filled me with shame.

In the silence, I waited for my father to give my mother a giant wink. It was what Lucy Ricardo always did on TV. Lucy turned her face to the audience, slipping her red-lipsticked mouth to one side of her face and giving a dramatic wink with her thickly eyelashed eyes. That wink told the audience that it was all a joke.

Instead, my father raised an eyebrow like a gun barrel. That gesture silenced my mother.

Numb, I flew from the table without finishing my meal. I ran out the door and jumped onto my bike, escaping to the shore, the one place that could always console me. But this time the sea failed to comfort. I closed my eyes. I could feel the stiff wind stinging my arms and salt air stinging my nose and the tiny streams that began as trickles slipping down my cheeks.

I tried to shut out the images. They were images of other eyes in another time and place. Those eyes melted into molten tears, and the molten tears ran down burned cheeks. I ached for those other eyes, willing them away from the source of fire, inviting them to plunge into the cool blue swimming pool before them. Instead, all I could see in my mind's sleepless eye was that searing image from *Hiroshima,* the image of those helpless Japanese lying at the bottom of a pool, its water evaporated, the people who jumped in to save themselves from the blast lying like boiled fish in the bottom of an empty kettle.

My fury knew no bounds. I faced a truth dropped on me like a blinding illumination: My father had been building not a swimming pool but a bomb shelter.

33

had returned to the lifeguard station again and again, for I had been writing more and more. Of course, a few of the poems on which I worked were for Mr. Henderson's assignment, but now many were for myself alone. Like the ocean itself, they had become for me both solace and escape.

Earlier that day I had stared at a bottle of Mercurochrome in my hand, hating my father, hating him almost as much as I had that day on the marsh, he in the bow and I in the stern in the canoe. Once the concrete that formed the sides had cured, he had become ever more obsessive about completing the bomb shelter. He had insisted that my mother and I spend all day Saturday helping him.

He directed us to perform specific tasks. To himself he assigned the task of hauling in the heavier items: oxygen tank, chemical toilet. To my mother he assigned the task of obtaining food stocks. To me he assigned the task of gathering a first-aid kit.

Ever since I realized that my father's plans were for a bomb shelter, not a swimming pool, I had even more trouble sleeping at night. Whenever I tried to close my eyes, the image of the Japanese streetcar swam again and again up into my consciousness. The car was jammed with people holding on to straps, their skin suddenly burned a reddish black, sitting or standing just as they had been before the bomb went off. Even when I finally slept, other images appeared—nightmares filled with freight trains hauling cargos of blood or flaming automobiles exploding like grenades. *Deliver us from evil.* Always on my lips were cries for God's protection. Not just for myself. But for the world.

That Saturday I placed the bloodred bottle of Mercurochrome into the first-aid kit. The kit now contained smelling salts and flimsy strips of gauze. I imagined the futility of postnuclear first aid: Band-Aids sliding off melting skin, smelling salts without the power to revive.

When I returned to the lifeguard station to write late that afternoon, I explored questions that agitated me: How could I ever come to terms with the bomb shelter? How could I ever understand the mentality of my father? How could I accept that gloomy future?

But I now recognized that Brenda had been wrong to question whether the Cold War was, indeed, a war. True, there were no troop movements, no blackouts, but it had turned everyone into a combatant, and every household was now on its front line. Staring into the bomb shelter, I saw that the foxhole, the K rations, the bunker had moved from the battle zones to the backyards. What use was a world that had turned itself into a garrisoned state?

As I confronted the bomb shelter, one fact stared me furiously in the face: I hated my father. Now watching my mother struggling to follow his orders, I wondered if she hated him, too.

Mother had been trying to overcome her disappointment, and I saw that she struggled to return to her familiar role of supportive wife. I watched her study the items of canned goods she had listed for the pantry shelves: potted beef, cereal, powdered milk, sugar. The list included the cans of lima beans I hated and the cans of corn I loved. I caught my mother checking the items off her list and sighing. Would she be able to give up her role as the calico-aproned Betty Crocker housewife and adopt the role of the lead-aproned postnuclear homemaker extolled for her knowledge of household decontamination procedures and her ability to make healthy meals from emergency supplies?

I admitted one important thing to myself: I missed Brenda Wompers. I longed for the antirobotic presence of those springy curls, that gap-toothed smile, the skewed tilt at the end of her nose. In the lunchroom at school, I overheard that she had given her UFO report and that her parents would soon press their protest against "under God," but the furious reaction I had expected from our classmates had not materialized. Perhaps I had been wrong about human nature.

34

On Sunday morning, the phone rang early, and its unexpected cry sent a shiver down my spine. I could piece things together only from my mother's side of the conversation, but when Aunt Minna appeared at our doorway followed by Uncle Bud, my aunt's face told me something terrible had happened.

Wills was missing. Aunt Minna had heard him go out late the night before to walk Gunner. This was something he did so often that she thought nothing of it. She must have fallen back to sleep, she said. When she got up for church, Wills wasn't in his room. Gunner wasn't around, either. Uncle Bud explained that they had searched the house and the neighborhood. They had even called Mr. Petty in hopes Wills might be at the pet store, but Mr. Petty hadn't seen Wills or his dog, either.

Aunt Minna paced back and forth across our kitchen floor. She had rushed to our house, not bothering to dress, throwing an old raincoat over her nightgown and replacing her bedroom slippers with the sandals she wore when she puttered in her garden. I felt guilty when I realized how little attention I had paid to Wills of late.

"Do you have any idea what happened, Genevieve?"

She had asked me a similar question years ago.

This time, I didn't know, of course. But I could guess. And this time, I would help.

The fog had just begun to lift over the jetties when we arrived at the boardwalk and crossed to the beach. As it was a Sunday morning, the beach was deserted, and I raced to the lifeguard station, my parents and my aunt and uncle lagging behind me.

I heard him before I saw him, his voice like the moan of a foghorn warning the ships at sea. It was a low, despairing call for help, the cries almost lost against the sounds of waves breaking against the morning shore.

From a distance I could see that they had strapped him to the roof of the lifeguard shelter, and Wills lay spread-eagled like a mattress thrown hurriedly atop a rickety truck cab.

"I'm coming, Wills," I cried. "It's me. It's Gen. Hold on. We're getting help."

Brenda's bells clanged ominously in the morning breeze as I took the steps two at a time. Then I saw that Brenda's anemometers lay strewn all over the station, broken in a mass of twisted wires and cracked gauges that looked like a sprung clockworks.

As I looked up at Wills, my eye caught the sight of

something black and furry hanging from the upper rafter. I moved closer and recoiled: It was the frozen body of Midnight, his tail stiff, his scratchy tongue hanging limply from his mouth. And far below me on the sand, scratching at a wooden supporting beam, sat Gunner, the blue-green feathers of Silver in his mouth, the neck of the feisty bird hanging limp and broken from the dog's muzzle.

Minna was the last one up the steps, hauling her padded body with difficulty up to the shelter.

Uncle Bud had reached for a pocketknife and was cursing as my father and he slashed the thick tape from Wills's arms and legs and hauled my cousin down.

I will never forget the image of Wills from that morning: the drool from his mouth was dried and salt-caked; the hair on his head slanted back from his face like the slats of sand fences in a storm; his arms and chest were bruised blue-black like jam stains across a toddler's bib.

Wills was dazed, confused. "Gunner," he whispered. "Where's Gunner?"

"Wills," I assured him, "Gunner's OK."

My words didn't register. "Gunner?" he repeated. "Gunner?"

"Yes. Gunner's fine. He's going to be fine, Wills."

After that, Wills's words came haltingly and out of order.

But what I pieced together was that he'd been snatched late at night on his walk with Gunner. Their faces had been hidden, but he had heard boys as well as girls, and one of the boys was big, as big as Brad Connors. They had stuffed him in the backseat of a car and driven to the beach with Gunner barking and thrashing like he did whenever he was caged. Wills had been terrified they might do something to Gunner. *Witches*, I thought angrily. When the car stopped at the beach, Wills hoped they might just dump him there and leave, but they had waited with him for what seemed like hours. *Devils*.

Eventually he learned that they had other plans. The other plans included dragging him across the beach. Wills had recognized the lifeguard station as they forced him, still blindfolded, up the steps. He believed it was early morning because he had heard clusters of seagulls flapping and diving as if for their breakfast catch. Soon the first set of captors was joined by others. These others threatened Gunner. They said Wills was to deny that story he'd told the papers last April, the one about the UFO sighting, the one that involved Janice, Iris, and Brad. Wills was to say he was mistaken, that he hadn't seen anything. If he didn't cooperate, it meant trouble for his dog. Wills said he must have passed out or been dreaming, for in addition to Gunner's constant barking and yelping, he heard more animal noises, sounds he recognized as the hissing of a cat and the squawking of a bird.

While Wills struggled with his story, my father cut down the cat and rushed to Gunner below. Helping the animal up the stairs, I saw that the spirited parrot had been taped to the dog's muzzle to make it look as if Gunner had attacked the bird. Reverend Steward's words floated back to me: Evil was indeed a presence in the world.

I looked at my disheveled, frightened cousin as Uncle Bud sat on one side of him, cursing those who had harmed his son, and as Aunt Minna stroked his hair, blessing the God who had returned him to her. Gunner lay on the floor beside him, licking his toes. Standing to either side of me were my two parents, ramrod straight, unbending. I knew I had never felt more alone. My father's eyes had seized on the features of the lifeguard station itself, taking in the word carvings in the wood: *pervert, Communist, radio-active.*

"Genevieve," my mother said, her voice issuing this warning: "You are not to breathe a word about this to anyone, do you hear? And you are to stay away from that horrid girl."

35

The pictures appeared in the *Easton Eagle* soon afterward. Of course, my mother's warning not to breathe a word to anyone hadn't mattered. To everyone in Easton, of course, seeing was believing. The photographs of the words carved into the lifeguard station confirmed the evil agendas of the enemies that occupied it: *radioactive, pervert, Communist.* The letters G and B outlined in cigarette butts confirmed membership in a cult. The candy-colored smears of melted candy were interpreted as notations in a secret code. The chicken bones left to rot and dry on the ledges implied wicked rituals in a satanistic cult. The bells, of course, were a kind of spectral accompaniment, a noisome music that supplemented the incantations and curses ringing out across the sand during midnight revels.

Most of the story in the *Easton Eagle* focused on the Wompers family. In a few short weeks their activities had become a staple of news in our little beach community. The story reported on the progress of their petition campaign against the Civil Defense curriculum and high-lighted their most recent protest effort: the attempt to have "under God" removed from the Pledge of Allegiance. The reporter explained that as soon as Mr. and Mrs. Wompers had presented their case at school to Principal Wrinkle, the principal had given them an angry refusal and then called the police to remove the Womperses forcibly from the school building. As the news of their latest crusade and the pictures of the lifeguard shelter spread throughout Easton, pickets began to appear outside the souvenir shop, and I realized that the Womperses' flagging business was finished.

But the focus of the reporting was not exclusively on Brenda and her parents, for it was my ninth-grade picture that accompanied the article and infuriated my parents. On the day the class photos had been taken, Brenda had not showed up for the photographic session. I now envied Brenda. I could now see the advantages of being such an antiestablishmentarian. The newspaper story itself, however, linked our two names: Brenda's through the anemometers and mine through the poetry notebook.

Lou Marchesco, the newspaper reporter, did ask me for my side of the story, but I had stared yet another fact in the face during this season with Brenda Wompers: Listening wasn't the same thing as hearing.

As far as staying away from that horrid girl, it wasn't difficult. Brenda had been suspended from school for yelling at Mr. Wrinkle while her parents were being escorted from school by the police.

On the day of Brenda's suspension, we had met one last time at the lunch table.

"Oh, dear, Genevieve. I'm so sorry," she said, putting down a slightly moldy piece of cheese. "I'm so sorry about the way everything turned out. For what happened to Wills. For all the pictures in the paper. For the discovery of the shelter. I know how much that place meant to you. To me, too. But to you especially."

I nodded. What she said was true. Somehow the shelter had changed irrevocably for me.

"I'm sorry, too," I said. "For what they did to Silver and to Midnight."

"That was cruel," Brenda seethed. "Just plain cruel."

I said, "I'm sorry, too, for all those ugly things they said in the paper about you and your family."

She shrugged. "In a way, I'm used to it. They said lots of ugly things in California, too."

She must have read the curiosity on my face. Then she went on. "Dad worked for a scriptwriter on *I Love Lucy* for a while. The scriptwriter was accused of being a Communist and was brought up before the House Un-American Activities Committee. And because my father worked for him, my father was accused of being a Communist, too."

I nodded, understanding completely. I had come to learn a great deal about guilt by association.

"Neither one of them actually *was* a Communist, of course," Brenda went on. "But they both lost their jobs, and then it was impossible for either of them to get any work in Hollywood. That's why we came out here."

"I didn't know," I said. "But that explains a lot." Still, it didn't explain why the Womperses insisted on stirring up trouble. To me, the Wompers family, including Brenda, kicked up dust unnecessarily; then they wondered why everybody complained of the coughing.

"Well, our family's tough about some things. But you, Gen. You're different. This is going to be much harder on you."

I wondered what she meant.

"People like you, people with feelings," she said, "suffer a great deal. Out of that comes their poetry."

I was taken aback. I knew I would have to think a lot more about what she said.

"But people who think a lot, people like me," she said, her head up, her curls doing their familiar, sprightly dance, "don't suffer as much from things like this. We tend to see the world as a comedy. Somebody famous once said it: 'Life is a comedy for those who think, but it's a tragedy for those who feel.'" Then she grinned. "It was probably somebody from California, don't you think?"

I heard the way she pronounced that word: Cal-i-*for*-nia.

I was grateful for all that Brenda had said. But I noticed that there were many things she had left unsaid: that she had caused all this trouble by presenting that material in her physics report; that there are good reasons to leave some scientific questions unreported, or even unexplored; and that science was not likely to provide the reasons for what happened at Salem.

Still, my whole heart ached. I would miss seeing Brenda Wompers.

36

While my grades in Algebra I plunged from high Cs back to Ds, at home my father continued his work on the bomb shelter. The construction manuals on the dining room table had been supplemented by catalogs from companies with names like Survive-ALL, Peace-of-Mind, and Secure-It. He had also acquired a substantial library of materials on bomb shelters with titles like *The Family Fallout Shelter* and *The Family Food Survival Kit*. With pride he bragged about the construction decisions he had made on the shelter's behalf. Because he had chosen double-walled concrete and steel joists, his shelter would be the very strongest possible: It would be unassailable.

My father and my uncle Bud worked on the shelter under cover of darkness, hiding their work from the neighbors. They rigged up lamps on poles to illuminate their work by night, and they covered the signs of their work with a tarp by day. Like the lifeguard shelter and my association with Brenda Wompers, I had to hide my knowledge of the shelter.

As the shelter drew ever closer to completion my father grew buoyant, but my mother's spirits deflated. While the concrete dried, she tried to shore up her Tupperware business. After the articles in the *Easton Eagle*, party cancellations became more frequent and invitations to bridge parties were abruptly curtailed. There were rumors that Mother would be asked to give up her presidency of the Welcome Wagon Club. As consolation, perhaps, she worked harder and harder on my confirmation dress, devoting time to it that she had previously lavished on her social and civic projects. Her goal was to create an underpetticoat so stiff that it would stand up on its own. While I stood before her bedroom mirror, the crinoline scratching my legs like sand at the beach, she nipped and tucked and hemmed and stitched.

I experienced twinges of sympathy for my mother, who seemed to be slowly changing. When packages for my father arrived from afar, her behavior was different. These packages came in enticing shapes and sizes from companies in faraway states like Nevada and Oregon. A circle like a hatbox. A square like a cake box from the bakery. A rectangle like a box for long-stemmed roses. At first, she eagerly watched my father open each new package. The hatbox contained a fan for blowing fresh air into the shelter. The bakery box contained a handheld Geiger counter with earphones to detect levels of radiation. The rose box contained a combination pick and shovel for digging out after the blast. As Mother saw the actual contents of the boxes, however, she lost her enthusiasm.

I missed Brenda Wompers. In my imagination we met up once more at the lifeguard shelter, holding our sides in laughter, mimicking the contents of my father's fallout shelter magazines. I imagined the two of us guffawing about the magazine advertisement for U-235 Atomic Shock Cure that looked and smelled like nothing more than baking soda and salt. I could see us hee-hawing over the photographs of the drawstring bags to yank over our heads in time of peril. I pictured us holding our sides at an article that recommended shaving the fur off the family dog or cat to keep pets from becoming radioactive. I imagined the two of us falling over with laughter at the catalog that offered the lead-foil brassieres.

At home my parents paid even less attention to me now, and one night I hiked to the beach alone, warming my feet in the sand and watching the white petticoats of waves rippling eerily at the edges of the black skirt of shore.

I stared up at the yellow globe of the full moon wishing Brenda Wompers had been right. I wished there *had* been a scientific explanation for Salem. As I watched the full moon pulling on the tides, I wondered if perhaps the moon had exerted some kind of celestial pull on the young accusers at Salem, sending them howling into lunacy.

In fact, I held an imaginary conversation with Brenda about it. "Since most of the accusers were young and just beginning to get their periods, the cycles of swelling, bloating, and bleeding might have been a perfect target for the influences of the moon, don't you think, Brenda?"

In this imaginary conversation, Brenda's eyes bugged out. She looked incredulous. "You mean *menstruation* might have caused them to see *witches*?"

I swallowed and reconsidered. Still, my theory outlined a different way of thinking about the problem. It might be improbable, but it wasn't entirely implausible, was it? Might it still be worth exploring?

Brenda looked entirely disgusted. "I actually didn't see how this could be possible. Next thing you know, Genevieve, you'll be suggesting that the teenagers at Salem saw witches because they had ESP or had been reincarnated or something equally silly. Or maybe the girls witnessed flying saucers landing at Salem, and they saw little green witches marching out."

I sighed, remembering our last real-world conversation.

After Brenda returned from her suspension, she had plunked herself down across from me at the lunch table, not saying a word.

Out of the corner of my eye I saw her pull a few wheels of cucumber from a paper bag and munch on them distractedly.

During the classes we shared together, we rarely looked at each other anymore.

I stared at my plate, ashamed of my molded Jell-O salad on a piece of lettuce.

I cleared my throat. "I'll bet you were glad to hear about Miss America," I offered, straining for a topic of conversation.

Now Brenda glared at me, her eyes like a blast at ground zero, wilting the lettuce and melting the Jell-O.

I gulped. She was right: It was an inane observation. Brenda wouldn't care a thing about Miss America. Even if she *had* come from California this year.

Brenda stood up and stomped away.

I was secretly relieved that I wouldn't have to think up any more stupid things to talk about. Both of us, I believe, knew that what had happened to Wills at the lifeguard station had changed things between us.

Now, looking heavenward, I knew that a scientific explanation for Salem was as unlikely as the notion that a man lived in the moon upon a surface of green cheese. The explanation lay in the unverifiable, unscientific story of the scorpion and the frog: Salem was in our nature.

37

escaped from home to the beach as often as I could now, for my parents were distracted by the work on the bomb shelter and the cold war raging between them.

It was the season of the fall called the marsh-hen tide, that season of full moon and high tide when the seawater flushes out the marshes. It was a season treasured by hunters, a season when the waterfowl are abundant, easy targets.

Biking along the marshes, I thought back to that time long ago in the canoe with my father, an October just like this one when the tides were high and the birds were plentiful.

I loved the nests of the marsh hens. The large nests floated above the high-water mark, made of interweaving grasses laced so tight that even the highest tide was unlikely to wash them away. Still, when water occasionally swept over the eggs, the birds, in their fierce loyalty, would drown themselves in an effort to rescue their young.

I knew the eggs, too, the plentiful fawn-colored globes

sprinkled with brown and purple spots. One determined hunter could collect hundreds of them on a single outing. And I knew the prostrate cries of the females when their young were stolen; so grief stricken were they that even their loyal mates stood mutely beside them, unable to offer a crumb of comfort.

Looking back to that long-ago October, I am still uncertain why I was even with my father that day in the canoe. I do know I was never chosen to share it again.

We set out early under the cover of darkness, when the morning was cool and the doves were cooing. It was the time of the marsh-hen tide similar to this one, when the grasses were crawling with hens and the waters with sportsmen.

My father was seated in the bow, and I in the stern.

It was a moment with my father like those I had witnessed before and since, a moment in which he, the huntsman, seemed a puny figure on the world's stage, swaggering across it with a rifle at the ready, enjoying an unfair advantage over a vulnerable natural world.

The tide was swelling the waters, advancing the boats, and the birds, hundreds of them swarming thickly like flies, scurried from hiding place to hiding place. The waters around me were bloated with fallen birds, felled by hunters before us. I shuddered as I dipped my paddle into the water, my oar knocking into their lifeless heads.

As we glided along the waterway, the noise was deafening, and the sound, to my sensitive ears, was one of sheer madness. Wings flapped like sheets in a gusting wind, and there was a lunatic chorus of mad splashes to escape, of caws and cries for help.

My father lifted his barrel, aiming at a thick covey in the tall weeds where the hens were huddling together in fear. Even at such a tender age, I recognized myself as a gentle Ferdinand, not a fierce matador. His rifle report rang out, and at the sound I panicked, standing up in the back of the canoe. *Deliver us from evil,* I prayed.

Then we instantly capsized, and I was gulping water and gasping for air. I was thrashing through the dead and dying bodies of a hundred hens, struggling through the muddy marsh to shore. As I threw myself onto the muddy ground, my eyes met those of a fallen bird. He was gasping like I was, his webbed feet paddling at the air, his neck convulsing. I watched as the light in his eyes glimmered, then faded into a lightless tunnel.

Now, looking into the sky, remembering that day, I watched a beautiful flock of waterfowl rising out of the marshes, fluttering in concert to the heavens.

I gazed at the horizon, at the ocean moving inevitably forward in wave after wave, longing for Brenda to be right, but my heart, like a drowning bird, seized on this truth:

> *. . . the world, which seems*
> *To lie before us like a land of dreams . . .*
> *Hath really neither joy, nor love, nor light,*

Nor certitude, nor peace, nor help for pain;
And we are here as on a darkling plain
Swept with confused alarms of struggle and flight,
Where ignorant armies clash by night.

When I returned home, slipping into the house by the side door, my father failed to see me. Having banished the catalogs and the building guides to a chair along the dining room wall, he was now staring instead at a hurricane map. It was spread out across the entire table, and I noticed the colored flags marching forward across the blue expanse of ocean.

My father muttered to himself as he fiddled with the placement of the green and yellow flags. "October fourth, the Windward Islands, already a Category Four. October fifth, east of Grenada, with winds clocked at ninety-eight miles per hour. October twelfth, Haiti is devastated." Then, speaking to himself alone, he added, "It's heading our way. I can feel it."

38

His hunch was right. On the fourteenth, the storm pulled sharply northward at an accelerated pace, and the red flags came out. As we prepared for Hurricane Hazel, my father was almost gleeful.

"It will be a dry run for the shelter."

"The shelter?" my mother asked.

"Yes, what better way to test its effectiveness than during a real disaster. Then we'll know what we need to improve on, what we need to add or change. It'll be like returning to the pioneer days," he said with uncharacteristic good humor. "Ah, yes, Martha. Like returning to a simpler time. When the family could all be together in a one-room cabin. Life pared down to its essentials." His snappy voice was like a smart pull on suspenders.

I caught my mother's frown. She didn't like life pared down to its essentials. She liked its complicated packaging, its abundant consumer choices.

The day before the storm was a frantic race against the

clock, for Hazel flew toward the Carolinas at a breathless pace. All over the county, the schools closed early so families could prepare for the storm. My father hammered up shelves in the shelter, and my mother listlessly lined up her canned goods and Tupperware bowls on them. My father finished the bunks that lined one wall, and my mother made them up neatly with blankets and sheets, but without enthusiasm. My father sighed with satisfaction and looked at my mother and me. "We've done a right nice job, ladies, don't you think?"

I shuddered, trying to imagine an existence with the world above the bunker either drowning in water during this dry run or bursting into flames during some future main event.

My mother sat silently with her chin in her hands.

"Did we leave anything out?" my father asked, looking around. With his nose he counted, checking off additional goods: the stash of incandescent bulbs, the fuses, and the nonelectric clock ticking loudly, like a Geiger counter. He checked off the presence in the corner of the Sterno stove and the jugs of bottled water, ten gallons worth, exactly what the Civil Defense instructor had recommended.

My mother wrinkled her nose, trying to think of an answer that might suit him. "No, I don't think so, George. I think you've thought of everything."

"Well, Martha," he said, puffing with pride, "I think

you and I and Genevieve ought to be able to pick out something to bring with us on this maiden voyage. Something special that you'd hate to leave behind."

I wondered what he could be talking about. I was certain my father was mad. If my whole world was dissolving above me, what could I possibly bring along for comfort?

"I can't think of anything," my mother declared. "You go first, George."

"Well," he said, "I'll bring my rifle." He produced it from under a bunk and held it aloft, proud as a homesteading pioneer.

"George!" my mother exclaimed. "Whatever could you possibly need a rifle for?"

Now he held the rifle to his eye and peered through the sight. "They say the first blast'll be the bomb itself."

Then he put the barrel down and looked at her. "The second blast, they say, Martha, will be the sound of folks shooting their neighbors. To keep them away from their shelters."

My mother's face turned down in a scowl. "George, you can't mean *our* neighbors, can you?"

What, I wondered, would be the point of life if you had to become a savage to survive?

My father shrugged, "God helps those who help themselves."

I bit down on my bottom lip, willing the words I longed to shout back down my throat. God? I thought.

How dare you invoke God's name in that way? God's commandment was to *help* your neighbor, wasn't it?

My mother now seemed to gain her footing. She was thinking hard, going back to my father's original question about what she might bring. She had lots of items to choose from. "Well, at first I thought I might like to bring the good silver, George." My mother's good silver was brought out on important occasions. Suddenly her eyes filled. "But I have trouble imagining my good silver at a time like this. Dining on potted meat and canned peas is such a waste of good silver, don't you think?"

I wondered if my mother's gift for positive thinking had finally failed her. As I studied her face, struggling to bat back the tears that had dammed up behind her eyes, I wondered if my mother, like me, had seized on the irony in the concept of our future "standard of living."

Now the dam burst and the tears flooded her face. "I just think," she said, blubbering and patting her chest, "I'll wear my Welcome Wagon pin and leave it at that, thank you."

My eyes traveled to my mother's chest. Mother was still wearing her Welcome Wagon president's pin, and I felt a shudder of pride.

My father only blinked before my mother's tears, turning instead to me. "What about you, Gen? What would you want to bring?"

I stared back at him and declared smartly, "Brenda Wompers. I'd like to bring Brenda Wompers with me."

My father looked at me the way he did over the breakfast table when I said that I wanted to wear lipstick to school or to stay up past midnight.

Before he could say anything, I had fled the shelter and had run to the beach to check on the Wompers family.

Mr. and Mrs. Wompers had hardly begun to make preparations for the storm. And they seemed in their own way as listless in their efforts as my mother. Brenda was nowhere around.

"What's the use, Genevieve?" Mr. Wompers muttered as I encouraged him to get their preparations under way. "The business is on the wane, anyway."

"I think we should just plan on moving to my sister's in Baltimore," offered Mrs. Wompers.

"You can think about that later," I said, urging them to take the precautions they had taken during Edna. I encouraged them to board up the windows and move the merchandise up off the floor. I made them a list: water, batteries, food. Alarmed, I heard them consider riding out the storm in their shop; relieved, I convinced them otherwise. "And you should get some sandbags," I added. "Mr. Petty's got a pile of them made up over at the pet store. He's offering them to anyone on the boardwalk who wants them."

Then Brenda burst through the door, a new kind of gadget in her hand. "Are you ready for that ride in the car?" she asked her parents, and then she stopped in her tracks, seeing me. Her animated face now flooded with joy.

"Oh, good," she exclaimed. "Gen can come with us now, too."

I didn't turn down the opportunity, but I can't say that I relished it. There was too much that needed to be done.

As we piled into the Womperses' rattletrap car, Brenda grinned broadly. "There's never a better time for an anemometer experiment than during a storm." When she smiled, I stared at the gap between her teeth and wondered if that was the secret portal through which all her brains slipped into her body.

As Mr. Wompers started the engine and it sputtered to life Brenda explained that she'd been studying something called the Beaufort scale ever since the Hurricane Hazel warnings had been posted. "The Beaufort Wind Strength Scale estimates the strength of the wind based on measurement *and* observation," she said, clearly delighted. "A Beaufort number of six, for instance, reflects wind speeds from about twenty-five to thirty-one miles per hour. That's the measurement part. At that number, large tree branches move and umbrellas are difficult to keep under control. That's the observation part. A Beaufort six is labeled a 'strong breeze.'"

The trip in the car involved another scientific experiment in which Brenda's parents enthusiastically participated. As Mr. Wompers drove, Brenda instructed him to watch the speedometer. He was to drive at exactly ten miles per hour. Then Brenda handed me a stopwatch and told me to time it for one minute exactly. Then Brenda instructed Mrs. Wompers to count as Brenda held one of her anemometers out the car window. The idea was to calculate wind speed based on miles per hour.

As we drove down the beachfront drive in advance of the storm we passed worried Eastoners busily hauling wood for boarding up windows and sandbags for sopping up the inevitable water. Brenda, however, hung out the window like a contented dog and never stopped talking: at a Beaufort number of 7, it is difficult to walk; at a Beaufort number of 9, shingles are blown off roofs.

I tried to warn all three of them about what I knew: that shorebirds had started to gather and cattle to wander; that dogs like Gunner would be lifting their ears and sniffing the air; that even nature's creatures from many miles inland were ruffling feathers and scurrying underground, alert to the danger. But my warnings fell on deaf ears, for the Wompers family had entered the world that was theirs alone.

39

The evening before the storm was expected to hit, Uncle Bud and Aunt Minna and Wills appeared outside the door to the underground shelter.

My father had seen them coming. He had run down into the shelter to fetch his rifle.

He leaned on his rifle as he looked over the group. Uncle Bud was holding blankets and gallon jugs of water. Aunt Minna had a Virginia ham under one arm. Wills was holding Gunner by a leash in one hand and his dog dish in the other. They were worried about their roof holding during the storm and assumed they could stay with us.

The wind had picked up, and my father looked up into the gunmetal gray sky. Then he lifted the rifle, holding it up to his eye and squinting through the sight at an imaginary target high above his head.

My father put down the gun and faced his family. "Sorry," he said, "this is a serious practice run. You can't stay."

I took in the stricken faces of our relatives. What was

he talking about? I wanted him to turn to me, to let his mouth slide to one side of his face, to stretch his lips downward, to let one eye give a big, broad, dramatic wink. Like Lucy. I wanted him to say that he was just kidding.

"Now, wait a minute, George." My uncle Bud stepped right up to my father. His burly frame was shorter than my father's, but Bud was strong. "Who was it spent all those nights helping you with that hole in the ground there?"

"You offered," my father grunted. He took the same tone with my uncle Bud that he'd taken with my mother. *I don't control what you believe.*

I saw Uncle Bud's thick hands rolling up into fists. Suddenly I wanted to scream.

My father kept his eye on Bud's hands and countered with words. "I thought the work you did over here was payback for all that work *I* did on your roof after Hurricane Carol."

Uncle Bud growled out an awkward acknowledgment.

Now my mother stepped up, the skirt of her apron blowing about in the stiffening wind. "You can't mean this, George. Of course they can stay. They're family."

"The definition of family grows very small during a nuclear disaster, Martha. There's limited supplies, limited air, limited everything."

Had I heard him right? What kind of life could be lived out in a doomsday rabbit hole that excluded even your closest family members?

My father swallowed. I watched his Adam's apple bob like a float on a fishing line. "Besides," he said, tipping the lowered muzzle of his gun in Wills's direction, "there's the dog."

"The *dog*?" Wills asked, bending down and throwing his arms around Gunner's neck.

"That animal nearly ruined our place in the last storm," my father announced. Then he turned to my mother for confirmation. "Didn't he, Martha"?

My mother's face was frozen. She said nothing.

"Well, now," Uncle Bud said, "we're surely sorry about that, George. But Wills wasn't with him then. And that dog's a peculiar critter. With Wills around, I expect Gunner will behave like a whole different animal."

My father studied the ground, deep in thought. He made circles in the dirt with the point of his rifle.

"Well, then," he sighed. "There's the problem of the boy."

"The *boy*?" Aunt Minna asked. Then she moved so close to Wills that the band of her gold wedding ring scraped across the metal of Gunner's dog dish. The scraping sound frightened me. So did the sight of my aunt huddled against her son.

My father kept his eyes on the ground. I saw patches of dust swirling and leaves scudding under his feet. "He's sick, isn't he?" asked my father.

Minna's pink face turned the pasty white color of flour.

"Well, we don't know yet, George. They can't tell. The doctors want us to come back so they can do some more tests."

"But polio's contagious," my father stated flatly. "Everybody knows that. Confined in close quarters together, we could all catch it. Gen here could wind up in an iron lung."

I tried to make sense of what my father was saying. I thought I had heard several things: that our family circle was too small to include Minna, Bud, and Wills; that questions about Wills's health squeezed the circle even tighter; that closed circles were facts that had to be squarely faced.

Everything I had learned that fall seemed to rise up from somewhere deep inside, and I stepped in front of my father, blurting out the words repeated so often over the television news reports since spring: "Have you no sense of *decency*, sir?" I said.

My father's head swiveled, and his eyes fixed on me like a bug on a specimen pin.

Suddenly I realized the source of the words I had spilled: They were the words of army attorney Joseph Welch when he confronted Senator McCarthy. I could have chosen no words of greater insult.

"Apologize, vulgar child," he commanded. His eyes were narrowed the way they were when he peered down a gunsight.

In my ear I heard the whisperings of Prufrock, that

weak and ineffectual attendant. He was challenging me: *Do I dare? and Do I dare?*

I heard the wind rustling the leaves of the cork tree. My feet began to stamp, my breath to snort. I was seized with an understanding: Definitions mattered; it was difficult to define *family* and *neighbor* and *God* and *poetry*, but the effort was important. I stared back at my father's tall, thin gray silo shape and the gun that bolstered his sense of power, and I realized that life was a series of defining moments: The definitions you chose made all the difference.

I turned to my family and said, "Let's all go in. We'll be just as safe together in the house."

They followed me, all of them except my father. Minna and Bud and Wills and Gunner and my mother. The breeze became a gale as we moved up the steps to the house. The tree branches shook and the windows rattled. But not one of us looked back.

40

We couldn't know exactly what time Hazel struck because my father had the shortwave radio and the nonelectric clock, but the electricity went out at four fifteen in the morning and we guessed that Hazel hit Easton with her full force between nine thirty and ten thirty A.M.

She struck at the worst possible time, for the full moon and the high tide guaranteed the greatest damage from rising water. What I had learned from Brenda's Beaufort Wind Strength Scale helped us gauge the progress of the storm as we listened from inside. When we entered the house the night before, I estimated a Beaufort 4, a stage in which thin branches shake and the breeze raises dust and paper. Throughout the evening we calculated the progress up the scale: twigs and branches breaking, Beaufort 8; shingles blown off of roofs, Beaufort 9; trees uprooted, power lines fallen, homes collapsed, Beaufort 10.

There were too many of us for the large hall closet, so we huddled in a corner of the living room like primitives around a campfire. With the power down, we lit candles, murmuring in the darkness. As the candlelight flickered across our faces Uncle Bud whispered stories of former storms. He reminded us of the dangerous shoals off Cape Hatteras known as the graveyard of the Atlantic. He remembered the great storm of 1899, seven vessels wrecked and sent to their graves off the coast. He recalled the legend behind the point of land called Hadnot Point: A four-year-old boy swept across the river during a storm had been saved only to find that he had lost the power of speech except for the single word *hadnot,* a word he muttered to the end of his days.

Listening to the sounds of the storm, my imagination echoed with the syllables of an e. e. cummings poem gone mad, and I heard the *thrashing, hammering,* and *whipping* participles slamming across my mind. I tried not to think of my father, riding out the storm in his nuclear bunker. Instead, I prayed. As the hurling horizontal fists of rain pounded at the boarded-up windows, as the wild wind whipped under the doorframes, I talked to God: *Deliver us from evil.* I reminded myself that prayers at a time like this were never misplaced. My prayers included Mr. Henderson and Mrs. Pagano, Reverend Steward and Raymond Donner, Mr. and Mrs. Wompers and Brenda. Especially Brenda. And, yes, even my father.

Whispering the prayers supplied a steady source of solace, as prayers always did.

Suddenly it was quiet. It was an eerie sort of quiet: like a fog-shrouded beach at dawn. Gunner rose from his haunches and sniffed the air. Aunt Minna stood on wobbly knees and pulled her blanket closer. Uncle Bud declared, "The eye. The eye is passing over. The first half of the storm is behind us."

And then we heard the frantic rapping at the kitchen door.

Now my mother stood, startled by the sound. She shivered and then headed out of the room. We followed her like obedient chicks.

It was my father. He wore a crazed look. He was soaked and shivering, trailing a wet blanket, the shortwave radio in one hand.

He could not stop babbling. "The shelter is filling with water! It has been rising all night! I have been left to drown!"

My mother took his hand, ushering him into the shelter of the living room corner. I heard his wet footsteps squeaking on the plastic runner.

Uncle Bud and Aunt Minna and Gunner and the rest of us left him to my mother, and we darted outside, impelled by curiosity.

The world beyond our door was as eerie as the marshes before daybreak. We saw salt spray covering the trees, giving them the appearance of frostbite. We saw sand replacing the soil in the garden. We walked with great difficulty into the backyard, wading through calf-deep water. We stared into the shelter and saw the soaked bedding on the bunks, a few empty water jugs dancing on the watery swells like life preservers, the Tupperware bowls juggling the currents. If the world ended, Tupperware would be eternal: It not only burped but floated.

"Inside, now," Aunt Minna cautioned, swatting the air with her hands. "Everybody in. The eye's likely to pass over soon. The storm's sure to start up again before we know it."

Through the doorway, I heard my father's sobs. I moved closer, and I saw his damp head on my mother's apron. Her fingers stroked his hair, and his words between sobs were both choked and hurried, like a child that was eating too fast. "Shhh, George," my mother whispered. Her voice was soft and quiet. Soon my exhausted father had fallen asleep, and Mother lifted his head from her lap. She began to busy herself, to adopt her familiar housewifely role. She bustled around my father, laying a towel across his hair; wrapping his damp body in clean, dry blankets; fumbling about in the dark bedroom to fetch him a fresh pair of socks. Her Welcome Wagon pin winked in the gray false dawn of the morning.

Then the wind and the rain returned in all their fury.

I heard the squawking of the radio and caught the wisps of news from far away: at Newport News the battleship *Kentucky* had broken its moorings and washed ashore. Someone at the weather bureau cited statistics about the Labor Day storm of 1935 that washed over the Florida Keys; with two-hundred-mile-an-hour winds and 408 lives lost, that storm was the only Category 5 hurricane in recorded history.

We shivered at this news and drew closer together. We felt for each other as protection against the gales prying at the roof and the tempest uprooting trees like a giant having a tantrum in a garden. Uncle Bud fiddled with the dials on my father's radio. "I hear something about Easton," he said, trying to tune the station in. We heard that the shrimp houses had collapsed like toothpicks, that a church steeple somewhere had broken off. We learned that 150-mile-per-hour winds had been clocked at Calabash, Holden Beach, Little River Inlet. We only imagined the rest: upended bumper cars at the amusement park, the Sweet Shop sign lifted from the boardwalk and dumped into Miss Simmons's flower bed, the mobile homes east of town smashed like Tinkertoys.

Still, together we were safe. We struggled to doze, our bodies leaning against each other on the carpet. I smelled Gunner's wet fur and wrapped my fingers around the soft handle of my cousin's ear. I was close enough to touch my mother's hands, intimate enough to hear the rise and fall of my father's breathing. With my family snoring around me, I sank into a dreamless sleep. Finally, as the storm passed over, I shook myself awake, grateful for our deliverance from evil.

41

The fallout from the storm rivaled scenes in Revelation. The shrimp houses had been tossed across the waterfront like scattered haystacks. Utility poles, their webs of hot wires sparking and crackling, threatened electrocution. Mobile homes had been flipped onto their backs like fish in a frying pan. Roadways had disappeared, buried under blankets of sand. Mature hardwoods as well as young pines had been uprooted. The pier was gone: Mooring lines with cables two inches thick had snapped like rubber bands, sweeping trawlers over seawalls and into town; now cranes in the middle of the streets lifted the boats in their maws like children's toys, preparing to set them back into the water.

But Hazel, like other witches, meant not just destruction; she meant death, too. Caskets in the graveyard had been unearthed by the storm surge, scattering bones of ancestors across lawns. I kneeled reverently beside a covey of marsh hens drowned in the floodwaters, aware that they were never seen inland unless blown ashore. As I whispered a silent prayer, something pink glimmered in the mud beside the hens. It was a conch, a Florida conch, a shell unlike any that was found around Easton. As I fingered the spiral shell in all its blushing pink humility, I marveled at its beauty and at the storm-tossed voyage that had brought it to me. Brenda had been wrong about one more thing: The more you knew, the *more real* mystery abounded in the world.

The strangest story of all was the way in which the Wompers family had been delivered from the storm. They, like our family, had ventured out during the eye of the storm, riding slowly through the high waters in their car, intent on surveying the damage. But they had been caught by surprise when the second half of the hurricane had roared up. They had not made it back into their house in time. Terrified, they were seized by the mad currents of water and flung across town where the automobile was blessedly lodged at the leeward side of the Easton Hotel on the beachfront. Trapped between the open carport and the back of the hotel, wedged in between the joists that held the carport to the roof, the car at first sheltered them from the surging waves. But then the waters inside the automobile began to rise, and Mr. and Mrs. Wompers and Brenda climbed on the roof of the automobile as the waters rose even higher. Just as they were about to be swept away, the steeple of the United Methodist Church floated by, bobbing like a buoy. They reached over and climbed on board, riding the rapids of waves as chairs from the diner, cages from the pet shop, and horses from the carousel at the amusement park swept by. The steeple had finally smashed into the center of the amusement park's Ferris wheel like a dart hitting a bull's-eye, and the Wompers family, like the wheel itself, had suddenly stopped spinning just outside Easton's city limits.

The weather bureau made it official: Hazel had been a Category 4 hurricane, packing winds of 140 miles-per-hour, with a storm surge of seventeen feet. The area had been flattened like Bikini Atoll. The world had come to hear about tiny Easton, North Carolina, for something other than the key rings and the bumper stickers of the souvenir shop after all.

Afterward, Brenda grinned and said she had three things to tell me. One, not one of them could swim. Two, she thought it possible that she and her family had been saved by the hand of God. Three, she would demonstrate her gratitude for my friendship before they left for Baltimore.

42

Things had changed ever so slightly at my house after the hurricane. It was as if a huge glacier had slowly begun to move. My father had not yet learned the difference between a father and fathering, and perhaps he never would. Still, at my mother's promptings, he was considering changing jobs. Mother said it wasn't healthy for a man to spend so much time staring facts in the face. She was even thinking of going to work herself. Her Tupperware business had largely collapsed, but my mother, thinking positively, had declared that strong business skills could be applied in nearly any workplace setting.

Both of them had even considered attending the Halloween costume party at the end of October. Parents were being included for the first time this year. My father had backed out at the last minute, but Mother and I had gone, and we had even helped each other dress. We had wrapped each other in aluminum foil, stretching some old vacuum cleaner hoses around our waists to feed into backpacks on our backs. We'd placed fishbowls over our heads that made our features look distorted through the glass. There was little mistaking that the two of us were almost-astronauts, Wonders of the Future. Mother had added the lead-foil brassieres as a kind of finishing flourish.

The hole in the ground that had once been intended as our nuclear salvation had been abandoned. Uncle Bud said it might make a nice wine cellar, and Aunt Minna suggested it might make a nice rec room for us young people, but my mother grabbed my sweatered arm and pulled me aside. "Let me work on your father," she whispered. "I don't think a pool's entirely out of the question yet."

Brenda's final act of friendship was one to rival the power of the storm. She hadn't breathed even a word to me about it, so I had heard only whispers from other classmates. When Brenda returned from her suspension, she had revealed just enough detail to raise everyone's curiosity. They had passed those details on to others in a young adult version of my mother's Gossip Game. Some students had even alerted the teachers to Brenda's forthcoming event, and the deep scowl Principal Wrinkle wore to school each day told me that his sour expression would only lift after Brenda Wompers had finally moved to Baltimore.

It was to happen at noon during the lunch hour on Brenda's very last day at Easton High, when more people would be free to attend. It would take place at her locker, in hallway 3B. Inside, I offered a silent prayer for Brenda's success.

At noon, hallway 3B was jammed with people. I saw that Janice Neddeger and her friends stood closest to Brenda's locker; they had arrived ahead of time to get the best view. Most of the other ninth-graders were there, too, and a few upperclassmen had ambled by, shrugging their shoulders and acting as if they had nothing better to do. But I was alarmed when I saw Mr. Wrinkle appear at the back of the crowd with a police officer at his side. And I was even more alarmed when I saw the reporter-photographer from the *Easton Eagle* pushing his way to the front of the crowd. In Easton rumors about the Wompers family spread as rapidly as kudzu in an open field.

With drama, Brenda checked the watch at her wrist. "Twelve noon, exactly," she said.

With drama, Brenda twirled the combination on her lock and then flung her locker door open.

With drama, Brenda reached inside her locker and pulled out some kind of a tool. It looked a bit like a gardening implement, like a pruner or a pair of garden scissors.

With drama, Brenda turned to Janice Neddeger. "Will you hold this, please?" Brenda asked. Then, just as the camera flashed, Brenda passed the tool into the hands of an astonished Janice Neddeger surrounded by her bouquet of friends.

With drama, Brenda raised her hand to her neck as if

she were a magician about to pull a rabbit from beneath her blouse.

With drama, Brenda slowly lifted, loop by loop, the chain from around her neck. And then she lifted the chain over her head.

With drama, Brenda held up the square face of the metal dog tag, passing it from left to right before the breathless crowd.

I gasped, instinctively reaching for the metal tag around my own neck.

"My snips, please," she requested of Janice Neddeger.

Janice jumped and passed the snips to Brenda.

With drama, Brenda then began to cut into the metal of the dog tag while the camera bulbs flashed over and over and Principal Wrinkle and the police officer rushed through the crowd.

Quickly everyone disappeared, scattering nervously into the warren of hallways like scared rabbits.

Afterward, there were pictures in the *Easton Eagle*. The story about Wills that said his illness had been diagnosed as a virus, not polio, had been shuffled to a back page. Plastered all over the front page were pictures under the masthead that read: PROTESTERS WREAK HAVOC AT EASTON HIGH; SEVERAL STUDENTS IMPLICATED. The picture showed Brenda taking the tin snips from the hands of Janice Neddeger while Iris and April and Renee stood at her shoulder like co-conspirators. I held my sides with laughter. I had learned that it was impossible to prove you were not a witch. I had learned that it was impossible to prove you were not a Communist. Soon Janice and her friends would learn that it was impossible to prove you were not a co-conspirator.

Aunt Minna surprised me. She invited Sally Redmond to come for my confirmation. Aunt Minna was aware that Brenda Wompers had left, and she thought I deserved some company.

The person who showed up seemed like a stranger. Had I forgotten how much Sally giggled? Had I never noticed the lisp that seemed like an affectation? And how had Sally adopted a New Jersey accent in such a short period of time?

Sally seemed to remember things about our friendship that I had entirely forgotten. "Remember that song we used to sing in front of my mirror?" she asked.

I tried to remember. "Was it 'Three Coins in a Fountain'? 'The Tennessee Waltz'?"

"No, silly," Sally said. "'Doggie in the Window.'"

She began to sing the lyrics of the song that had been so popular last year:

How much is that doggie in the window?
Arf! Arf!

The one with the waggly tail?
How much is that doggie in the window?
Arf! Arf!
I do hope that doggie's for sale.

Sally enjoyed this song much better than I did. When she sang, she rolled her eyes pleadingly, like a puppy, and made eager *arfing* sounds. Watching her, I felt silly.

Sally reminisced about our Lucy-watching two Januarys ago. "Don't you remember, Gen?" she asked, tugging at my arm.

I stared blankly at her. I'd forgotten this, too.

"You know, the episode when Lucy delivers her baby."

"Oh, yes," I nodded. I remembered. "Lucy was pregnant," I said.

Sally looked shocked. Like she'd stuck her finger in an electric socket. "Not *pregnant,*" she said. "Ex-*pect*-ing."

I swallowed, finding the memory distasteful. What came most vividly to mind was my father's snorting over the newspaper soon afterward. "More people tuned in to that TV episode about the birth of little Ricky Ricardo," he groused, "than they did to the presidential inauguration of General Dwight David Eisenhower."

I stared into the round, open eyes of my all-the-way friend.

"Remember how we'd raided the refrigerator that time, Gen?"

307

I did remember one evening with Sally in her kitchen.

"Lucy was having cravings. She was hungry for the oddest things. She made herself a concoction of all kinds of weird things. Sardines and hot fudge. And pickles and ice cream, I think. And we went to my refrigerator and made ourselves the very same thing. Remember that?"

Standing at the back of the church, preparing to make my way down the aisle, I ran my right toe up and down against my left leg; the petticoat itched. Mother had achieved her victory: It was starched so stiff, it managed to stand up on its own accord. Preparing to march to the front of the church, I noticed the way the light filtered through the stained glass, wavering and blurry like the search for an answer to a difficult question. I stared at the leather-bound copy of the Bible in my hand, and I wondered about Brenda's final gesture. Was it good fruit? Or corrupt?

I couldn't be sure. If I had learned anything from Brenda Wompers, it was that things weren't easy to define. Poetry was somehow all of the definitions and none of them. All at once. The same with God and all the other complicated things I had struggled to define this fall. Words were just words, in the same way atoms were just atoms. Like Brenda said, it all depended on how you put them to use.

As I walked down the ocean blue aisle of the church, I felt as if I were sailing into a whole new world. I experienced a lightness I had only ever experienced in water. It had been a stormy year, one that had drenched the steeples and drowned the cocks. Still, as I moved past the faces of family and friends smiling at me from the pews, I was certain that I knew the answer to at least one question: I knew who was my neighbor.

Later, after I told Sally good-bye, I stood before the mirror in my room, Brenda's parting gift to me in my hand. I lifted it onto my head, angling it first to the left and then to the right. Suddenly I realized I never had found a word to describe the moment when you first felt like you can trust another person, but I had learned that some things didn't have words attached to them. I saw that the beret seemed to bring out the color in my cheeks and loaned my serious face a jaunty air. I thought back to something Mr. Henderson had said and extended it even further. What applied to poetry also applied to people. You never understood them entirely: You just nudged out a little understanding one piece at a time. I smiled back at the girl in the mirror. Perhaps tomorrow she might wear the red beret to school.

A Time Line of the Cold War

May 7, 1945   Germany surrenders, ending World War II in Europe.

July 17–
August 2, 1945   At the Potsdam Conference Germany is divided into four military occupation zones by the victorious allies with France, Great Britain, the United States, and the Soviet Union each administering a zone. Berlin is similarly divided; the French, British, and U.S. zones are located deep within the Soviet zone.

August 6, 1945   The United States becomes the first country to use atomic warfare when it drops an atomic bomb on Hiroshima, Japan.

August 9, 1945   The United States drops a second atomic bomb on Nagasaki, Japan.

August 14, 1945   Japan surrenders, ending World War II.

1945–1950   Soviet-influenced communist governments take control of much of Eastern Europe including Hungary, Albania, Poland, Eastern Germany,

Czechoslovakia, Romania, and Yugoslavia creating, along with the Soviet Union, the Soviet Bloc. As the Soviet Union expands its sphere of influence it is increasingly viewed as a threat by the U.S. and other Western countries.

March 5, 1946   Winston Churchill, the Prime Minister of Great Britain, introduces the term "Iron Curtain" to describe the division between Western Europe and the area controlled by the Soviet Union in a speech at Westminster College in Fulton, Missouri.

July 1946   The United States tests an atomic weapon on Bikini Atoll in the Pacific Ocean.

June 24, 1948   The Soviet Union begins the Berlin Blockade, cutting off all highway, river, and rail traffic to Western-controlled West Berlin to force the Western powers out of Berlin.

May 12, 1949   The Soviet Union lifts the Berlin Blockade after it fails to drive out Western powers.

June 1949	The Chinese communists under Mao Tse-tung defeat the Chinese Nationalists.
August 29, 1949	The Soviet Union tests its first atomic bomb in Kazakhstan.
October 1, 1949	Mao Tse-tung proclaims the People's Republic of China, and soon after begins negotiating a treaty with the Soviet Union.
February 9, 1950	Senator Joseph McCarthy claims he has the names of 205 communists in the United States State Department in a speech to the Republican Women's Club at the McClure Hotel in Wheeling, West Virginia. This ushers in the "Red Scare." He continues making accusations of communism through 1954.
June 25, 1950	The Korean War begins when North Korean forces allied with the Soviet Union and China invade democratic South Korea, and a United States-dominated United Nations coalition comes to the aid of South Korea.
January 12, 1951	The Federal Civil Defense Administration is established to help

ensure that Americans are prepared for nuclear attack.

September 24, 1951	The Soviet Union conducts its second nuclear test, an improved plutonium bomb.
November 1, 1952	The United States tests its first hydrogen bomb over the Marshall Islands in the Pacific Ocean.
November 4, 1952	Eisenhower is elected president of the United States.
June 19, 1953	Julius and Ethel Rosenberg are executed for passing atomic secrets to the Soviets.
July 27, 1953	The Korean War ends, leaving the border between North and South Korea roughly where it was before the war started.
March 1, 1954	A second American hydrogen bomb is tested on Bikini Atoll, and the *Lucky Dragon* incident occurs in which a crew of Japanese fishermen are accidentally exposed to radioactive fallout.
April 22, 1954	The United States Army versus Senator Joseph McCarthy hearings

begin. McCarthy's staff is accused of pressuring the army to give favorable treatment to a friend. The televised hearings last 36 days and expand in scope as accusations and counter accusations mount.

May 27, 1954   Nuclear scientist and chairman of the United States Atomic Energy Commission J. Robert Oppenheimer has his security clearance revoked after having been accused of having communist sympathies.

June 14, 1954   Congress adds "under God" to the words of the Pledge of Allegiance to distinguish the United States from the officially atheist Soviet Union.